Haunted
New Hampshire

Thomas D'Agostino
Photography by Arlene Nicholson

Schiffer ®
Publishing Ltd

4880 Lower Valley Road, Atglen, PA 19310 USA

Dedication

This book is dedicated to my mother, Yvette D'Agostino, who always loves my stories.

Other Schiffer Books by Thomas D'Agostino:
Haunted Rhode Island

Designed by John P. Cheek
Cover design by Bruce Waters
Type set in Decade/Souvenir Lt BT

ISBN: 0-7643-2573-6
Printed in China

Published by Schiffer Publishing Ltd.
4880 Lower Valley Road
Atglen, PA 19310
Phone: (610) 593-1777; Fax: (610) 593-2002
E-mail: Info@schifferbooks.com

For the largest selection of fine reference books on this and related subjects, please visit our web site at **www.schifferbooks.com**
We are always looking for people to write books on new and related subjects. If you have an idea for a book please contact us at the above address.

This book may be purchased from the publisher.
Include $3.95 for shipping.
Please try your bookstore first.
You may write for a free catalog.

In Europe, Schiffer books are distributed by
Bushwood Books
6 Marksbury Ave.
Kew Gardens
Surrey TW9 4JF England
Phone: 44 (0) 20 8392-8585; Fax: 44 (0) 20 8392-9876
E-mail: info@bushwoodbooks.co.uk
Website: www.bushwoodbooks.co.uk
Free postage in the U.K., Europe; air mail at cost.

Contents

Acknowledgements

I would like to thank my wife, Arlene, who not only took all the photographs in this book, but also planned and drove to all the sites.

A very special thanks to Karen Mossey and The New England Ghost Project, Raven and Ghost Quest Paranormal Society, the Lake Winnipesaukee Historical Society for their list of haunted places, Merrianne Weston with Jennifer Lerz, and everyone else at the Three Chimneys Inn, Zhana Morris of The Music Hall in Portsmouth, Pat Rockwood, David Smolen and the rest of the New Hampshire Historical Society, Carolyn Tremblay of the Dover Public Library, New Hampshire Department of Health and Human Services, David Emerson of the Conway Historical Library, Vess Liakas of the Windham Restaurant, Jon Randall of the Country Tavern, The staff of Tortilla Flat, Tamika C. Harrison, Amy Patryn, The Appalachian Mountain Club, Catherine and Jose Luis Pawelek of the Beal House Inn and Restaurant, Fiona Bloome at Hollowhill.com, The Tuck Museum, Andrea Card, and Eleanor Porritt of the Goffstown Historical Society, Stacey Brooks of the Strawberry Banke Museum, Martha Wilson of the Mount Washington Hotel, Lianne Keary, and Kimberly Swick Slover of Colby-Sawyer College, and mostly my mother Yvette D'Agostino, who supported my dream and listened to endless hours of my ghost stories, and my father, Rudolph D'Agostino, for letting us be what we wanted.

Introduction

According to research submitted by paranormal investigators over the years, New England is arguably the most haunted area in the United States. Among the New England states, New Hampshire was said to rank rather low in overall haunts. Maybe it is not so much that it is barren of spirits, as it is that the residents just consider them another part of the New England charm that the Granite State exemplifies so proudly.

Having some of the oldest Colonial structures in America, New Hampshire can certainly boast about its ghosts. And, as you will soon find out, there are a lot of them to boast about.

In the following pages, you will read about pirates, buried treasure, spirits who do not realize their time on this earth has long since come to a close, and the power of the devil's deeds on nature and man. You will also visit haunted restaurants where the ghosts walk among the living, a jogger who still runs his ethereal course, phantom soldiers eternally holding their positions, Neolithic astronomical calendars put here long before European colonies were ever feasible, and Indian spirits that take vengeance on the encroachment of their sacred land.

Sound like a page out of a book of fantastic journeys into another world? Well, welcome to New Hampshire, a magic place, where everyone loves to visit over and over again. And in some cases, have never left—even in death.

Grab your map and some courage, for the spirits await to give you a tour of the Granite State. Who knows, maybe you will find a lost treasure buried near a rocky beach with the help of a ghost, or solve the mystery of the stone circle in North Salem. Even if you don't, you will not soon forget the stories and places that are about to unfold in front of you.

Special Note: Though specific locations may be given for haunted locations, it is not my intent to invite you to visit without approrpriate invitation or authority from the establishments involved. Some sites are located on private property, others are visibly posted, discouraging trespassing. Please take the appropriate measures to insure both your safety and legal responsibilities. Always maintain the necessary respect for the locations (and inhabitants, living or dead) at these sites.

Alton

Alton Town Hall: The Building With the Most Town Spirit

The town hall in Alton, New Hampshire is a very busy place, both during, and after, business hours. Alton is a beautiful little town along the Southeastern shoreline of Lake Winnipesaukee. The area was originally called New Durham Gore when natives of Roxbury, Massachusetts settled there in 1770. Knowing that they could not name the area Roxbury, they decided to name the town Alton, after a prominent family that was part of the band that had relocated. Alton was eventually incorporated in 1796.

The boundaries of this delightful little settlement include Wolfeboro Harbor, the largest of the islands along the Southeast end of Lake Winnipesaukee, and the town itself. Alton is considered to be the birthplace of the Mount Washington Cruise, as the first side-wheel steamboat of the famous tourist attraction paddled away from the docks of Alton in 1872.

Oddly enough, the town has not become the metropolis one might think, despite its charm, attractions, and scenic vistas. The population stands at about 3,493 people, which makes it a rather sparsely settled parcel of land for its size. This count, however, does not include the number of ghosts roaming the Alton Town Hall.

The hall is relatively new to Alton. It was built in 1894 at a cost of $15,098. The brick edifice and clock tower loom over the center of town at a height of eighty-five feet. The four-faced clock is named after Thomas E. Howard and has hands that stretch over three feet in length. The clock still strikes every hour on the hour since its construction. But it is the twilight hours that the tolling becomes an ominous call for the spirits that once occupied the empty rooms. It is *their* moment to live once again within the walls of the town building that was a large part of their life-long past.

The tower is one place that has had spirit activity. It seems that someone still climbs the stairs to the clock tower to check it periodically. Staff members have heard footsteps on many occasions, after hours, ascending the stairway to the ancient timepiece. Could it be the ghost of Mr. Howard checking on his memorial namesake? Most think not. Instead they lean towards the probability that it is the spirit of Arthur Twombly, a former longtime Selectman of the town and entertainer of sorts in the 1920s. Mr. Twombly regularly hosted a movie and dance soirée in the upstairs auditorium during his lengthy tenure as Selectman of Alton.

Tourists and townsfolk alike flocked to see a motion picture of the day, then pitched in to move the chairs so the orchestra could set up. The rest of the evening was reserved for dancing and merriment. It appears that they still keep their vigil in the old ballroom to this day.

Former Police Chief Tom Mynczwor once stated that he stopped counting the strange phenomena that constantly occurred in the building. One particular night, officers proceeded to the third floor to investigate voices and footsteps that permeated the otherwise silence of the closed building. Once upstairs, they found chairs lined up in the hallway as if someone was having, or just had, a crowd seated in them. They called in the police dog to investigate. The dog became a bit unnerved and began to whimper and cower. They all could feel a presence in the area, and the dog made their fears more realized. They sealed the building and performed an intense search for intruders as protocol. The search revealed that they were the only occupants of the building at the time. Living occupants, that is.

The chief is not the only one to experience the strange incidents in the town hall. Former Town Planner Glenn McLean attested to the voices and footsteps heard after hours on the third floor. He has called out many times, thinking fellow employees were in the building with him. He has also ascended to the third floor to investigate, only to find an empty room now void of voices and movement. The third floor is where Mr. Twombly held his gala events. The auditorium once had a balcony where people could view the stage from up above. The auditorium and balcony have since been modified to serve as a courtroom for the town. The stairway to the clock tower is just past the old auditorium. Many think the voices and footsteps are from the ghosts of past revelers who found escape from their daily routine with the cinema and dancing. They still flock in the eternal gathering that frequently interrupts the placid quiet of the aged structure.

Former clerk Gwen Jones became a believer within a few short weeks into her employment. She was working late one night when she heard a door open near hers. She thought it was a co-worker who was also burning the midnight oil, so she went to say hello. Oddly enough, there was no one in the room. She checked the building, but found no one else. Every room, as well as the front doors, had been locked tight. She soon became accustomed to the voices and footsteps as she fulfilled her long tenure as Town Clerk in the haunted building.

Pat Rockwood, present clerk at the town hall, stated to me that people still hear the voices and footsteps from the third floor to this day. Present staff at the town hall also reported furniture moving in the old auditorium area. They say it sounds like chairs being shuffled around—as if someone was cleaning up after a gathering. Lights have also been known to turn on and off with no visible hand to manipulate them. People have even heard doors mysteriously open and close from time to time. Maybe some of the spirits occasionally become bored with their endless dancing, and shy from the ethereal gathering to meet new people.

The Alton Town Hall is located at One Monument Square, P.O. Box 659, Alton, New Hampshire 02809. Take Interstate Route 93 to Exit 20, Route 3 towards Winnisquam and Laconia. Take Route 11A to Route 11 South into Alton. Monument Square is also Main Street. You will see the town hall when you get into Alton Center.

Alton Town Hall and clock tower where spirits still celebrate in the revelry of the past.

Auburn

Devil's Den

Imagine being part of the New Hampshire Forestry Management. There you are, sitting in a tower at Mine Hill in Auburn looking out over Devil's Den. It is early evening, and dusk has enveloped the hilly area as the stars start to rise from their hiding place behind the peaks. Suddenly, you see something in the den below. What you see resembles strange balls of moving light. Could they be flashlights? No, because they do not cast a beam. Lanterns? No again, because they appeared out of nowhere and seemed to be dancing. Ghost lights? Yes! You would not be the first to have witnessed them. Many rangers, volunteers, and even sightseers to the area have witnessed the strange balls of light that they have dubbed "Ghost Lights."

Ghost lights are seen all over the world. They are usually white or yellow in color. They resemble small globes or candle lights as they bob up and down on their eerie journey along the landscape. Sometimes they may appear bluish or red, and look more like a blast from a blowtorch than a ball of light.

These enigmas have made scientists and paranormal investigators scratch their head in a puzzled manner since the beginning of time. They are identified by a lot of different names, like will-o'-the wisp, ignus fatuus, corpse candles, and even jack-o'-lanterns to early viewers of the phenomenon. There are a host of other names, as well, depending on the country or origin of the witness to these strange glowing orbs.

Some say they are death omens, while others have found them to linger in an area where a tragic event took place. Some cultures believe them to be the lights of an invisible funeral procession wandering along the ethereal trails to nowhere. Many scientists have explained them as marsh gas, electrical energy that has taken form much like ball lightening, or even energy rising from the earth itself. In the end, no one knows for sure but the invisible entities carrying the lights in their never-ending journey through eternity.

The ghost lights of Devil's Den are said to be evil. The den is reportedly afflicted by the malevolent glow. According to witnesses who have been close to the lights, they seem to have been affected by demonic visions during the duration of the phenomena. There are also drastic temperature changes while in the presence of the ghost lights.

The tower, operated by the Manchester Water Works, was taken down in the 1990s, but those brave enough can still trek through the area of Mine Hill into Devil's Den to perhaps spy the legion of the ghostly glow as it roams by.

Devil's Den is located at Mine Hill. Take Route 101 to Exit 2, Chester Road South. Go past the town hall and stay right at the fork of Chester Road and Bunker Hill Road. Mine Hill is about one mile from the fork.

Benton

Mount Moosilauke's Evil Ghost

As we ascended upon the peak of Mount Moosilauke, the famous words of Mark Twain echoed in my head: "If you don't like the weather in New England, wait a minute." The dark clouds began to swirl overhead as the sound of thunder rumbled in the distance. Storms move fast in these parts. One minute the sky is blue and serene. Then, out of nowhere, howling winds and pelting rains force unsuspecting hikers to seek immediate shelter. No wonder there are so many lost each year to the unforgiving mountain ranges.

My two hiking partners and I knew that setting up a tent in this weather was futile, for we would surely be blown off the summit by the furious winds. We retreated in haste to an emergency cabin near the barren summit of the mountain. Soon, the storm was wreaking havoc along the mountainside. Lightning lit up the peaks like a shower of flares in the sky. The bombardment of rain and thunder made it impossible to talk at less than a shout. The winds rocked the cabin to and fro on its stone foundation. Although it was held in place by heavy cables, we still feared the steel cords would snap. This fear was not as punctuated as the idea that Dr. Thomas Benton might be making his rounds on such a nefarious night. If he lurked in the darkness, waiting for one of us to spew forth from the cabin, we certainly would have no clue, as the howling winds and torrential downpour were deafening.

Who is Dr. Thomas Benton, you ask? Well, the White Mountains are full of strange stories and legends of ghosts and spirits that are hardly rivaled. The scariest thing about these stories is that most of them actually happened. In the case of Dr. Thomas Benton, it still goes on.

Young Thomas Benton was a precocious lad. He was a very intelligent boy to say the least. The Bentons were among the first settlers of the White Mountains along with other families, such as the Oakes and the Richardsons. In the early 1800s, Thomas schooled in a one-room schoolhouse typical of the day before traveling off to practice medicine.

He returned to his hometown a full fledged Doctor of Medicine. All was well. He even became engaged and sought a bright future for himself and his fiancé. Plans, however, were short lived. According to accounts, his fiancé died of typhoid fever, and in his despair, Thomas retreated from his practice to a mountain cabin that he had built for seclusion. The cabin was located at the summit of Mt. Moosilauke and was secured by heavy cables anchored to the rocks. He took a trunk that contained apparatus willed to him by one of his favorite professors while in medical school. The contents of the trunk held a lifelong quest of all the equations and experiments that the old man had been performing in order to create an elixir of youth. The distraught Dr. Benton would soon be destined to continue where his mentor left off.

It is often said that playing God can turn a man into a monster. The madness of the mind can become uncontrollable for the quest of immortality. That is what may have happened to the good doctor. He completely disappeared from the community. Not too long after, local farmers began to notice that their livestock was either disappearing or found dead of mysterious circumstance.

The troubled residents deduced that the reclusive Dr. Benton had something to do with it. Several men pooled together and hiked up to his cabin. Once inside, they saw remnants of experiments they could not perceive—yet no sign of the doctor. They waited for a while, then exited back down the mountain before the darkness crept in. While on route, one of the posse fell behind and vanished from sight. When he did not return, a search was made for him. They found his body the next day on the mountain. The only sign of harm was a strange cut behind his left ear.

Fear began to fill the townsfolk. Experimenting on animals was one thing, but humans? Word got out that babies from nearby towns were disappearing—kidnapped while they slept. It was concluded that Benton was stealing the toddlers for his experiments on immortality. The once friendly and amorous doctor was now the devil's concubine using the blood of the young and innocent for his elusive serum. One day, as a woman was in her yard, a man with long white hair and a black cloak ran up to her young daughter and snatched her away into the woods. A band of men led by the daughter's father followed the footprints in the snow along Tunnel Ravine to a cliff. There they saw the mad doctor holding the girl high. The men pleaded for him to release the girl and he did. Right off the edge of the cliff. According to accounts, he was never seen again.

In the 1860s, the Tip Top Hotel was built at the top of Mount Moosilauke. People were afraid to stay on the foreboding mountain despite the fact that the evil doctor had not been seen in thirty years. No one wanted to be the next victim of the crazed mountain man. Before long the apprehension died down and the hotel began to flourish.

Reports of a shadowy figure in a black cloak darting among the trees became more and more frequent. As the twentieth century rolled around, the wicked wraith of Dr. Benton was still seen wandering the mountainside, supposedly searching out victims for his elixir. Could it be that he actually conquered death? Some say he did, and still wanders the mountaintop waiting for an unsuspecting victim to wander from their group. If that is the case, the wicked doctor is now two hundred years old.

The Tip Top Hotel now lies in ruin after being destroyed by fire. Some blame it on Benton. There is a place called the Ravine Lodge at the base of Mount Moosilauke where guests can stay and enjoy the view of the mountains as well as family-style meals served piping hot. They also might catch a glimpse of a dark shadow moving through the trees.

As for the cabin I once stayed in on the summit, there are those who say it is the original cabin where Dr. Benton held his experiments. Others have told me this cabin was a newer cabin built on the foundation of the original. Either way, the shelter was taken down in 1978—supposedly for safety reasons. Maybe so, or maybe there are other reasons why such a necessary shelter would disappear from the mountaintop. Then again, they never stated what the safety reasons were. Based on what is presented here, let's allow *you* to be the judge. If you decide to stay at the Ravine Lodge or hike the mountain, keep all eyes and ears alert. That twig that snaps in the woods or that shadow you think you just saw just might be that of the good doctor getting ready to pay you a house call in the dead of the night.

Mount Moosilauke is located between Benton and North Woodstock. The Ravine Lodge is at the eastern base of the mountain. Take Exit 32 off Interstate Route 93. Turn right onto Route 112 West. Travel about three miles to Route 118 and turn left onto that road. Travel 7.2 miles to Ravine Road and turn right there. Travel to the end of the road and reverse direction in the turnaround. Drive back down and find a parking space on the right side of the road closest to the lodge without blocking any part of roadway. Trailhead to summit can also be reached from there.

Boon Island

Boon Island Lighthouse

As cameras flash away from the rocky bluff of Cape Neddick, capturing the scenic wonder of the Nubble Light, it must cross some tourists' minds as to what that shimmering shaft in the distance, barely larger than a needle in their camera lens, is. Little do they know that they are getting two lights for the price of one. The silhouette on the ocean's horizon is the largest light tower in New England, situated seven miles out to sea. It is called the Boon Island Lighthouse and is associated with one of the most tragic stories of ghosts and hauntings in the North Atlantic.

Boon Island is a small rocky outcropping off the coast of New Hampshire and Maine. Some say it belongs to New Hampshire—a warning near the Isle of Shoals—while others insist it is property of Maine. Let's go with the New Hampshire buffs for now. Read on as I tell you about one of the most forlorn places in all New England.

Its desolate location makes it a very hard place to get to, much less fueling any desire to reside there. Nineteenth century Lighthouse Superintendent Samuel Adams Drake wrote of the lonely island and its perilous location, describing the rock as that of a prison when the storms of the Atlantic wash over the top of the island. He goes on to say that the island is so remote, that when there is a storm, there is no way to escape to the safety of the mainland. Thus, those who choose to keep the light are always subject to suffer the perils of the untamed sea.

The island got its name in 1682 when the *Increase* slammed into the hunk of rock. The crew was stranded for only a short time. Four survivors were rescued when someone saw smoke signals coming from the fourteen-foot-above-sea-level land mass. They viewed the sparing of their lives from the ruthless sea as a boon from god.

On December 11, 1710, the *Nottingham Galley* became the second known victim of the rocky protrusion. This crew was not as fortunate as those of the previous wreck. Two died on impact and the remaining crewmembers struggled to stay alive, finally resorting to cannibalism after three weeks on the island.

Following their rescue, provisions were frequently put on the island to prevent future casualties of possible shipwrecks. Recently, nine cannons were found near the island that belonged to the *Nottingham Galley*.

It wasn't until 1797 that Lighthouse Superintendent General Benjamin Lincoln was able to convince the Boston Marine Society to put a beacon on Boon Island. President John Adams had the final say, and in 1799, an eighty-foot beacon was erected for the sum of six hundred dollars. Light keepers were sheepish to tend the beacon, as it was not very safe. Their fears were substantiated several times as storms destroyed the light on numerous occasions, before it was totally swept away during a gale in 1804.

In 1805, a stone beacon was erected for permanent safety, but the curse of the island did not ease up. Several of the workers drowned in a boating accident shortly after leaving the island. According to Celia Thaxter, author of the book, *Among the Isle of Shoals* (1873), a man related to her how he had grown up on the island and once found some bones among the rocks. When he brought it to the attention of his parents, they told him how the workers capsized while attempting to leave the barren rock. One washed ashore near Plum Island, while the surviving worker buried the others there on Boon Island covering their remains with many boulders that had since washed into the sea. The remains were moved to York for proper burial, but maybe their spirits still linger looking for a way home as well.

Like the previous lights, that one succumbed to the ravages of the sea. In 1811, President James Madison put forth $3,000 to have a better light put on Boon Island. It stood only thirty-two feet high. Because of the dangerously low level of the island, the first light keeper lasted about two weeks. He hastily retreated to the solitary pile of rocks, citing that the waves would cover the whole island and the light would sway from side to side. By 1831, the island was barren of a light once again due to the storms and brutal north winds of the Atlantic.

The trouble with keeping a beacon on Boon Island was coupled with shipwrecks. In 1846, the schooner *Caroline* smashed into the remote atoll. Nathaniel Baker saved all aboard and was commended for his bravery, despite his release as light keeper in 1849 due to political favors. The situation on Boon Island was a grave one, but soon the present light would make its way into maritime—and haunted—history.

In 1852, building began on a mega-light that would stand the test of time. By January 1, 1855, a 133-foot masonry tower shone brightly from the little island. The cost for the tower and the lamp was an astonishing $44,973. This did not snuff the island's curse. Many locals tell the story of the lady in white who roams the little isle. Fishermen and visitors, as well as keepers of the light, have seen the forlorn spirit along the rocky edge of Boon Island.

She is said to be the ghost of a light keepers wife. The young couple had been recently married when he'd accepted the position as light keeper on Boon Island. The remote location of the island was, at first, like a honeymoon getaway, but soon the young man took ill. When he was too weak to climb the stairs to the light, his wife would leave his side to make sure the wicks were proper and the lamp was well lit. She would then rush back to his side to tend to him. She knew someone would be out to check on them soon, but unfortunately a great storm kicked out of the north, and the gale force winds held all sea travel at bay for several days.

The husband suddenly took a turn for the worse and died during the brunt of the storm. His grieving widow could only keep the light lit and wait for the storm to pass. For a week, she constantly ascended the 168 steps to the light, carefully trimming the wicks and keeping the light burning in a valiant effort to warn any wayward ships of the impending doom the island was now famous for.

It wasn't until after the storm passed that people along the shore saw the light was not lit. Some of them gathered together and rowed out to the island. There they witnessed the young woman staggering along the rocky edge, driven insane by grief and exhaustion. She died shortly after they found her. Now her ghost stays behind on the island, still watching over ships passing by as she faithfully fulfills her duties in the wake of her beloved husband's demise. Her spirit is fated to eternally warn the mariners who pass the light, making sure no one else shall ever be stranded on the lonely pile of rock so once aptly called Boon Island.

Boon Island is located about seven miles off the coast of New Hampshire and Maine. It can only reached by boat. Those who are brave enough to want to visit the island can go to the website www.boonisland.com for more information.

Bretton Woods

The Mount Washington Hotel

Martha Wilson, Resort Public Relations Manager at the Mount Washington Resort at Bretton Woods provided me with the following write-up about their famous ghost. It truly is a shining example of ghostly behavior.

A SHINING EXAMPLE OF FRIENDLY SPIRITS

Bretton Woods, New Hampshire

The reality of The Mount Washington Hotel's resident specter is a benign entity that is most commonly recognized as the "Princess." Her presence is the result of a wonderful love story for a remarkable man and for the edifice he built as a testimony to his success and his eternal passion for his wife.

Carolyn Foster was the daughter of a prominent Boston meat merchant. Many chefs from New Hampshire's grand summer hotels visited his Quincy, Massachusetts market stalls for the finest cuts of meat their discerning guests came to expect. Carolyn summered at one of these hotels, the Twin Mountain House, and happened to meet the industrialist-turned hotelier, Joseph Stickney, at one of the many summer social events. Stickney had made his fortune in railroading and coal, then returned to his native New Hampshire in his senior years to try his hand at the hospitality business. He purchased the Mount Pleasant House located where the Lodge at Bretton Woods now sits. Joseph was immediately smitten with Carolyn. She was a very popular young lady and possessed much charm and tact according to the society writer of a New Hampshire newspaper.

In the fall of that same year, Joseph sailed his yacht, the *Susquehanna*, from New York to Boston. He invited Carolyn and some of her socialite friends to join him for a dinner cruise around the harbor. From then on, he wooed her incessantly until she fell hopelessly in love with him and agreed to become his bride.

The couple honeymooned at Stickney's chateau in France, resided at his townhouse in New York, and spent summers at the Mount Pleasant House in New Hampshire's White Mountains. How they enjoyed the summertime! Carolyn was quite the sportswoman and loved to swim, play tennis, and take long walks along the river with her beloved Joseph. Always the visionary, Joseph imagined owning a second hotel on the plain between the Mount Pleasant and the western slope of Mount Washington. It would have magnificent views in every direction and he would build it with every modern amenity to be the finest of all the grand hotels. With the architectural expertise of Charles Alling Gifford and the skilled craftsmanship of 250 Italian laborers, the Spanish Renaissance Revival behemoth became a reality as it opened its doors on July 28, 1902.

Special indulgences were incorporated for Carolyn. An indoor swimming pool filled with the curative waters of the Ammonoosuc River and tempered with jets of steam for her comfort; an ornately decorated and distinctively feminine private dining room where she could entertain her social peers in style, a private courtyard fern garden, and a secret stairway that accessed a mezzanine perch where Carolyn could spy on the goings-on of the busy lobby. From behind the secrecy of a sheer drape, Carolyn would observe her guests making the descent of the grand staircase on their way to dinner. Only after all of her guests were seated, would she ready herself with the finest fashions and jewels of the day. Night after night she would make her grand entrance through the lacquered mahogany and Tiffany stained-glass doors to be the finest dressed and bejeweled of all the ladies in the room. To her guests, it was uncanny how she could never be outdone.

Whenever she traveled, legend has it that Carolyn insisted on sleeping in her own bed. The ornate hand-turned maple four-poster bed that she and Joseph shared would be carefully dismantled and reassembled for voyages abroad, or for their regular visits to the exclusive Jekyl Island Club in Georgia. Joseph and Carolyn spent the hotel's second summer season in France. Joseph's health was failing and he wasn't up to entertaining guests. In December 1903, at the age of 64, Joseph left Carolyn a young and deeply sorrowful widow. According to a New York Times obituary, the cause of death was a "stroke of apoplexy." Carolyn continued to operate the hotels and returned to The Mount Washington the next summer. But alas, the vivacious young woman had grown markedly sullen and withdrawn. So great was her love for Joseph, that Carolyn commissioned a stone chapel—"a church by the side of the road accessible to everyone of every nation and creed." A memorial to her beloved Joseph, the Stickney Memorial Chapel still stands as a testament to her devotion to this very day.

Carolyn returned to France, where she mourned her husband's death in solitude. A decade later, she met and married a French Royal, Prince Aymon Jean de Faucigny-Lucinge. The wedding took place in July of 1913 at London's Westminster Cathedral. It was most likely for her social standing that a woman of Carolyn's position and age would marry so well. The couple continued to operate the New Hampshire hotels as well as lodging properties in Switzerland and France. Upon her return to The Mount Washington Hotel, and for the rest of her life, the staff and hotel guests alike, referred to Carolyn lovingly as the Princess. In August 1922, she was widowed again but carried on with her summer visits to New Hampshire. Ever watchful of the hotel operations, the Princess attended to her guests' needs and although she hired a competent manager and staff, was involved with all business decisions. Every night she joined her guests for dinner in the Hotel's elegant dining room—always at the same table just inside the doors and to the right.

Having no children by either marriage, when she died in 1936, the Princess bequeathed the New Hampshire hotels to Reynolds, a Harvard Business School graduate and Rhode Island Hospital Trust Banker. Her final wishes included the construction of a mausoleum, where she and Joseph could be reunited in death. A Tiffany stained-glass depiction of the view from the Hotel's South Veranda toward Crawford Notch reminds respectful family members of the couple's devotion to each other and to the idyllic setting they had loved and shared.

Tough times had befallen the grand hotels as automobiles became more popular and summer vacationers turned to new motor courts and roadside attractions. Unable to maintain two grand hotels in such close proximity, Reynolds had the Mount Pleasant House razed in 1939. Joseph and Carolyn's surviving palace had also fallen to ruin and closed at the end of the season in 1942. It changed hands several times until a group of New Hampshire businessmen purchased the structure in 1991. They may own the hotel at present, but it is the Princess who staff and hotel guests continue to experience as the presence that keeps a most watchful eye over the property.

Chief of Security Fred Hollis remembers the years when the hotel closed for the winter. "One time, when I was making my rounds on a night when there was a full moon, I was walking into the ballroom—which I had done on many occasions before—and got about halfway across the ballroom floor when every hair on my body electrified. I mean it tingled! I had the strangest feeling of a presence. I couldn't go any further. There's really no explanation for it."

Now embarking on its sixth year of welcoming guests on a year round basis, the hotel continues to provide "sensitive" visitors with an assurance that life may indeed continue after death. Visions of a woman dressed in Victorian elegance are occasionally reported. She is most often seen in the hallways on the guestroom levels of the hotel. Visitors report the sound of a light knock on their doors, only to discover no one there. Personal items suddenly disappear then reappear in the exact place of their loss, sometimes days later.

The experience that is most commonly reported, and oddly enough affects people most individually, occurs in one specific guestroom. Only a small collection of the hotel's original furnishings survived the numerous changes of ownership since the Princess's passing in 1936. However, one of those rare surviving pieces was the lovely hand-turned four-poster bed that traveled the world with Carolyn. It now graces a spacious guestroom on the third floor and offers guests a restful night's sleep ... or sometimes not. Several guests staying in room 314 have reported being awakened during the night by the sensation of some-one sitting on the end of the bed. Many report waking to the sight of a woman sitting there, brushing her long hair as she looks thoughtfully into the darkness of the room. Most guests who report strange goings on are not frightened by their experiences.

The benevolent specter, whether real or imagined, seems to pose no threat. It would appear that in death, as in life, Princess Carolyn is very connected to this magical and romantic place known as The Mount Washington Hotel. She seems curious about the operations of her visionary husband's legacy and continues to be involved in the daily duties of her role a century later. Certainly, she and her beloved Joseph are pleased with the loving restoration and continued commitment to guest satisfaction that the current owners, management, and staff of their magnificent hotel have asserted. For more information about The Mount Washington Resort at Bretton Woods, please call 877-873-0626, toll free, or visit www.mtwashington.com.

There you have it folks. The only closer first hand story a person can experience in regard to this haunted hotel would be if they stayed a night in it themselves. It is highly recommended.

The Mount Washington Resort at Bretton Woods is located at Route 302, Bretton Woods, NH 03575. Take Interstate Route 93 to Exit 35, Route 3 North to Route 302 East.

Center Ossipee

Raccoon Mountain Road

America's early traveling days were certainly a dangerous undertaking. The small horse paths and sparse population made for a very perilous journey at best. Indians, wild animals, and dastardly rogues stealthily hid among the trees and brush that lined the trails and rough roads of the countryside. Innumerable voyagers of these roads met a tragic end while making their way from one place to another. Some were never heard or seen again, while others, as in this next case, are still eternally wandering the roadway looking for peace. The strange thing about this next story is that the wanderer is not a person, but a horse.

This spectral animal once belonged to gristmill owner Adam Brown. Sometime during the 1830s, Mr. Brown was traveling Raccoon Mountain Road, towards his residence, on his trusty steed. It was more than likely that he was carrying a healthy sum of money from his daily toils at the gristmill. He never made it home. Adam Brown was ambushed and killed while on route to the safety of his domicile. During the attack, his horse panicked and ran. The poor horse also suffered a terrible fate, for it fell into a ravine and became badly injured.

With no one around for miles to help, the poor horse starved to death. Mr. Brown was found and given proper burial, but it seems the horse was overlooked as it lay in the ravine hidden from the road. Now the spirit of the horse haunts the area of its demise. The phantom steed can be seen following visitors who trek the eerie thoroughfare. The ghost appears out of nowhere and seems to beckon the witnesses towards him. Then, without warning the wraith is gone. The horse looks so real, people have tried to pet it, only to have their hands pass through the animal before it vanishes into thin air.

Perhaps the animal is leading them to where it fell into the ravine. It could be looking for peace by decent burial, or perhaps looking for forgiveness because it ran, leaving its master behind to suffer such a horrible fate. No one knows for sure why it is eternally trotting the area of Raccoon Mountain Road. If only ghost horses could speak...

Raccoon Mountain Road is located near the town of Center Ossipee. Center Ossipee is on Ossipee Lake in Eastern New Hampshire. Take Interstate Route 93 to Exit 23, Route 104 into Meredith. Take Route 25 and follow it past Moultonborough. Follow into Moultonville where Routes 16 and 25 meet. Near Moultonville Mill Pond Bridge, bear north onto Raccoon Mountain Road.

Concord

Siam Orchid Restaurant

Concord is the capitol of New Hampshire. It resides in Merrimack County in the lower eastern part of the state. When it was first settled in 1659, it was called Penacook based on the Indian name "Pannukog" which translated means crooked place or bend in the river. The town was incorporated as Rumford in 1733, but was later changed to Concord in 1765. This was due to a nasty dispute over town boundaries between Rumford and neighboring Bow. It did not become the state capitol until 1808. The State House was built in 1818, and is the oldest continuously-used state house in the country. Another achievement Concord can boast is the building of the famous Concord Coach, modeled after King George III's coronation chaise. For those who need help rising in the morning, they can thank the city of Concord. Levi Hutchins of Concord invented the first alarm clock there in 1787. There are many museums and historical societies, including the New Hampshire Historical Society. There is much to see in Concord. You might also spy a ghost or two if you visit the right places.

One such place is the Siam Orchid Restaurant on Main Street in Downtown Concord. The spirits of the Siam like to move objects while diners watch in awe—particularly drinking glasses. Mysterious voices are heard from the dining room as well as the kitchen. The otherworldly sounds emanate out of nowhere when the areas are void of living souls. They are barely understood, though defiantly audible.

A number of patrons have turned quickly to see who might be giving them an earful, only to find that there is no one behind them to cause the voice they just heard. No one that can be *seen* anyway. Even the staff has heard voices call out to them when working in the kitchen. Sometimes, several might turn at the same time towards where the sound originates, only to find that there is no visible being in that area.

Not only is the building home to the eatery, but there are living quarters above it. Tenants above the restaurant have heard the voices in the dark hours of the night, long after the last of the staff have gone home. They also claim to have been awoken by the moving of heavy objects in the Siam. Upon investigation, the boarders have found that the restaurant was silent, dark, and all the doors were locked tight. Once again, upstairs they would be subject to the eerie sounds of phantom furniture being moved around below them.

The restaurant is part of a small chain that hosts other locations in Manchester, Gilford, and Durham. These locations do not seem to have ghostly activity going on within *their* walls. The Concord locale was the first one to open for business. Maybe the ghosts are finicky and will only reside

The Siam Orchid Restaurant.

in the real thing. The Concord was the first, the oldest, and the one worthy of their nightly shenanigans.

Dine there, and if your glass slides across the table or you hear disembodied voices coming from behind, you know you are being visited. Maybe you could tell them of the other restaurant locations in New Hampshire. Perhaps they might like to stop in and compare.

The Siam Orchid Restaurant is located at 158 Main Street, Concord, New Hampshire 03301. Take Interstate Route 93 to Exit 14, Route 9 (Loudon Road) towards State Offices. The restaurant is on corner of Route 9 and Main Street.

Margarita's Mexican Restaurant

This restaurant building, located in the heart of beautiful downtown Concord began its life as a defender of the law. It was built in the early twentieth century to house the police, jail, and courthouse—all in one. With the growth of Concord, it became necessary to expand the facility into separate operations. Thus, the building became outdated.

In the early 1970s, the structure became Chuck's Steak House. It was known for its excellent food and "spirits" almost immediately after the restaurant opened. People came from all over to witness the ghosts of the establishment move dishes, place settings, and even empty their drinks when they turned away for but a fleeting moment.

In 1984, it became Tio Juan's Mexican Restaurant and Watering Hole. General Manager John Pelletier purchased the restaurant the following year and established a chain of eating places called Margarita's Mexican Restaurant. In keeping with the chain, Tio Juan's became Margarita's in 1999. This has done nothing to slow down the playful and sometimes pesky ghostly activity.

The foyer host greets patrons in the original witness box that once sat in the courtroom. The courtroom is now a lounge where people from all walks of Concord can relax and have a drink. The use of the former trappings left upstairs is rather inventive, but it is what lies on the lower level that is intriguing. There are sixteen jail cells that have been transformed into little dining areas. They are called dining cells and are painted in a bright mural fashion depicting life in Mexico.

In the thirty plus years as a restaurant, the staff has seen much. There is one particular spirit named "George" who has a signature set of pranks. The staff has actually witnessed his moving furniture and table settings. The patrons are not deprived of the regular phenomena as George likes to entertain them by moving chairs in the dining room—sometimes while they are still seated in them! Staff members hear voices coming from the empty dining cells long after they have been cleaned for the night. Decorations on the cell tables tend to disappear or get thrown into the aisle.

It would appear the ghosts of Margarita's like to interact with the living. The customers seem to enjoy the company, as many come to the restaurant in hopes of a chance encounter with the playful spirits. Who were these residual entities that give the customer more than just a great dining experience? No one really knows for sure, but there were many people jailed in those cells, and a few even died there. Others had their fate sealed in the courtroom, and still others may have loved their duties as officers of the law so much that they never left their posts.

If you should find yourself at the restaurant and turn around for a second only to have your drink emptied or someone slide your dinner plate away from you, don't be afraid. For many years customers have shared food and drink together at the canteen with those they can see—and those they cannot.

> Margarita's Mexican Restaurant is located at One Bicentennial Square, Concord, New Hampshire 03301. 603-224-2821. Follow directions above but bear left onto Main Street. Bear right onto Pleasant Street, then take the next right onto Warren Street. The restaurant in on left. You can also park on Main Street across from Warren Street.

Margarita's Mexican Restaurant. It was once the town police station and courthouse as noted on crown of building.

New Hampshire State Hospital

The New Hampshire State Hospital is a well-maintained multiplex of buildings that span over 160 years. The first building was erected in 1838. It was originally called The Asylum for the Insane. It became an established institution in 1842. Soon after, the name was changed to the more dignified title of the New Hampshire State Hospital. It was the seventeenth mental care hospital in the United States and the seventh such establishment in New England.

Its motives and manner of treatment has evolved with modern medicine and knowledge of mental illness, but its intentions remain unchanged: to treat patients who are suffering from any kind of mental state that inhibits them from continuing a fruitful progressive lifestyle. Most of the admissions are involuntary and therefore confidentiality has preceded any other information on the hospital and its history.

Despite the vague history of the hospital, there were a few staff members who were willing to at least share the ghostly occurrences within the facility. Activity is limited to the old original building of the complex built back in the early nineteenth century. Very few staff members are brave enough to carry on any length of tenure in that building. Those who have had a brush with the restless ghosts of the old section are ill at ease when having to enter the building—for any reason.

Many of the people within the hospital have heard footsteps in the corridors after hours. When they peek down the spans to see who might be the source of the noise, the hallways are empty and become eerily silent as the tapping of heels trails off into the void. Elevators start up by themselves. When they reach their destination, the doors slide open as if some invisible occupant has reached the end of his or her ethereal journey. The doors then close in a normal manner, but the elevator does not continue on its way. No one knows when a living being will emerge from the shaft or when the hair on the arms and necks of bystanders will begin to stand on end as a ghostly rider silently brushes out of the elevator. The entity then moves unseen to its otherworldly destination.

Quite often the staff will hear footsteps descend upon them, then stop abruptly. They might turn around and see that there is no one behind them, or they might even be watching in alarm as the hall is void of a living visible entity. Yet they hear the sound of someone walking towards them. Cold spots are common during these ghostly occurrences. The cool air either moves around or stays in one place.

Most of the time the ghosts choose to be invisible. They do show themselves by way of pushing papers and files off desks and tables from time to time. No one knows who is causing the phantom phenomena. Early insane asylums were full of tortured souls and untimely demise. It could be a number of lost spirits still wandering in agony or even the ghosts of former staff members who were once prisoners themselves as witnesses to the horrible conditions of early mental treatment. Maybe they are living an endless torture trying to right the wrongs of the last century. Or maybe they are just making their eternal rounds forever, assuring themselves that every patient is safe and secure, for all time.

New Hampshire State Hospital is located at 36 Clinton Street, Concord, New Hampshire 03301. Take Exit 14 off Interstate Route 93. Take a right onto Bridge Street. At the second light, turn left onto Main Street. Proceed past the Capitol building to the next light. Turn right onto Pleasant Street. At the second light, bear left onto South Street. At the first light, bear right onto Clinton Street. The entrance to the hospital is on the right, just past the District Court. This is a private hospital. Permission will most likely be needed to roam around the grounds.

Conway

The Phantom Snowmobile

When I was teaching near the Connecticut border some years ago, one of my students told me about the phantom snowmobiler. I inquired to others about the strange tale and heard a few accounts of the ghostly rider. Connecticut residents seem to know the story pretty well. Now you may ask, what does Connecticut have to do with New Hampshire ghosts? Well, I will relate the story as best I can remember. You see, the ghost that rides the trails of Conway in New Hampshire originally hailed from Connecticut.

According to the story, a family named Prudeator, or Pudeator, once farmed the Nutmeg State. There were six burly sons and their mother. They all married and had children. They were not rich, but one of them got an idea to buy a snowmobile. This was back in the 1950s, and snowmobiles were the newest and latest modern mechanical wonder. They pooled their money together and purchased the vehicle.

They had a friend who owned a cabin in Conway. He told them that the snow trails and ridges went as far as the eye could see, and then some. That was all they needed to hear. They loaded the snowmobile onto their trailer and towed it up to Conway. The convoy reached their destination in the afternoon and unloaded the snowmobile. They were several miles from the actual cabin, but the fields were ripe for fun and speed. The mother went on to the cabin by herself to prepare victuals for the sons when they returned. This was not to happen. While taking in the fun of their new toy, a blizzard hit with full-mountain intensity. The trucks would not budge from their icy domain and the brothers were forced to spend a few days and nights surviving the storm.

Here is where the story takes a twist. One account states that, after the storm, the brothers got the trucks out of the snow and proceeded to the cabin where they found the mother frozen to death from the bitter cold. She had run out of wood during the Nor'easter and could not get out to salvage more. They solemnly strapped her to the snowmobile, as there was no room in the cabs of the trucks for her to ride. During their trip home they stopped and took in some food and drink. Upon leaving the diner, they noticed the trailer was gone. Whether they even hooked it up correctly or it was stolen is an eternal mystery. It was never seen again—and neither was mother.

The other version states that one of the brothers went off with the machine to get help but never returned. He, somehow, lost his way in the blizzard and he, along with the snowmobile, was never seen again.

Either way, the phantom snowmobile now makes its rounds through the fields and trails of Conway. On dark snowy nights the echo of an engine from another world can be heard in the wind, and a faint ghostly light is seen moving through the distance. No one knows if it is Mother Pudeator or the unfortunate son endlessly searching for rescue from the icy storm that held grip on the family. They only know that when they see the ghostly vehicle, it is best to stay put within the warmth of the home, or risk suffering the same fate.

Conway is located in Eastern Central New Hampshire at the junctions of Route 16 and Route 112, better known as the Kancamagus Highway. You can take Interstate Route 93 to Exit 32, then proceed on Route 112 East.

Stark Road

Conway was strictly Indian territory until 1765, when settlers began to migrate to the area. Joshua Heath, Benjamin Dollop, and Ebenezer Burbank came and built log cabins in what is now Conway Center. Daniel Foster joined the small band of settlers in 1766. He settled close by in a place that was forever called Foster's Pocket. The place is still there, only a Northway Bowling Alley now graces the spot where his cabin once stood. The town slowly grew and grew until it was divided into villages.

General John Stark served in the Revolutionary War. He was a hero in the Battle of Bennington. He is also credited for the state's motto "Live Free or Die" as it first appeared in a statement he wrote in regard to the Revolution. Major Samuel Stark and Captain William Stark served selflessly for the colonies in the French and Indian Wars. William and Samuel Stark, along with Lieutenant Hugh Sterling, fought gallantly for Roger's Rangers. For their bravery, they were all awarded land grants in what is present-day Conway. Stark Road and neighborhood was born. Lieutenant Sterling married Isabel Stark, sister of Samuel and John Stark. As the family grew, so did the land.

Isabel was a fearless woman. Her husband once fell seriously ill, and she took it upon herself to hunt for food. She went out and killed a buck, then proceeded to skin it. As she was dragging it back, she heard the growls of a wildcat. She dropped her take and climbed a tree. Soon a bear showed up, and a fierce battle ensued. The animals killed each other. She climbed down the tree and went home, returning the next day for the meat and skins of all three animals.

When the Stark family died, they were buried in the family cemetery on Stark Road. As time went on, other names graced the small graveyard. Soon, the Stark family began interring their loved ones in the Center Conway Village Cemetery. Other families who were using the graveyard began to follow suit. This might have caused some unrest for those already interred in the family lots.

At night, the graveyard glows with the spirits of those who are perhaps looking for their loved ones. Those who are buried there are Samuel and Rebeckah Stark, along with their daughter, Melinda, who died at the young age of twenty. Hugh and Isabel Stark are not buried there, but their daughter, her husband, and their daughter, Nancy, are.

A child, who died February 19, 1870, at one year, nine months, and eighteen days of age sits alone in a grave, as the rest of the family is interred in Center Conway. Other such names show that the families buried the deceased there, then, for some reason, sought to be buried somewhere else when their time came. There are several family names that occupy a sole plot, as the others were moved to Center Conway. Even General John Stark, who died in 1812 at the age of seventy-two, was relocated to Manchester.

There are twenty-six stones in all. Some are damaged from roadwork that took place in 1982. Maybe this lends to the haunting of the cemetery. It is also said that eyes watch people as they proceed down the road by the cemetery. Could they be those of the interred, making sure that no one else causes further damage to their markers? If so, then leave well enough alone.

There is also another true story that is associated with the area of Stark Road. A young lady was in love with a man who was living in the neighborhood. She died of a broken heart after finding out that he was repeatedly unfaithful to her. On her deathbed she cursed the lands of her husband's family, saying that their cleared farms would grow with weeds and vines, and the soil would never yield another crop. They should never prosper again from their toils of the terrain. So true to the day lives this curse that one can drive down Stark Road and see the woods and brush that was once acres of fruitful farmland. Who exactly were the man and woman? The names of the couple have become hazy through history and time. Some of the interred in the Stark Road cemetery might hold a clue to this mystery. Do not be afraid to ask, if you go there. Also, do not be surprised if you get an answer.

Stark Road runs from Route 302 just outside Center Conway to Crystal Lake Road. The area can be reached by taking Exit 40, Route 302, or Exit 32, Route 112. Both are off Interstate Route 93.

Crawford Notch

The Willey House

Crawford Notch, New Hampshire is nothing short of spectacular. Today, it is a tourist attraction full of hiking trails, scenic train rides, skiing, and incredible views of the White Mountains. Also, there sits in the middle of the notch, the remains of a truly curious New England tale—the foundation of the tragic and famed Willey House.

The history of New Hampshire's famed notches is a tumultuous one. Benjamin Willey's book, *Incidents in White Mountain History*, vividly depicts the perils of tradesmen sledding goods through the dangerous notches, and tourists who bravely traversed the snow laden trails while death lurked 2,000 feet above in the form of potential landslides.

Crawford Notch is such a place. One would leave the Crawford home at the entrance of the notch and travel thirteen miles through the crevice before the next home, the Rosebrook place, came into view.

That is, until a man named Henry Hill built a little inn in the center of the notch. Travelers finally had refuge from the elements during their long trip through the indenture. The only problem was, voyagers of the notch were too few and far between for Mr. Hill to make a decent living at his public house. He was forced to abandon his scheme.

Enter Samuel Willey Jr. In 1825, he, his family, and two farmhands moved into the abandoned farm and began renovating it. Repairs to the weather beaten house, barn, and shed took all winter, but the work paid off as spring showed new promise to the homestead. The ever-present overhanging crags, some 2,000 feet above the house, still gave the family an uneasy feeling that disaster was always looming over their heads.

The family and guests huddled around the fireplace each night after dinner and took console in the Bible. Many a weary traveler found much comfort in their ritual, and sometimes, a new faith. In June of 1826, the earth broke free from above, sending a landslide off to one side of the house. Then another loud rumble, and a portion of the mountain slid to a halt on the other side of the house. This was truly a frightening scene, but was soon forgotten and passed off as a once in a lifetime occurrence.

The summer rolled on fair and hot. August 28, 1826, started like every other day, yet the air was eerily still and the animals had grown strangely restless. Soon the sky became dark, as thunder echoed through the mountains.

The time had come!! The fiercest storm to hit the notch barreled down upon the area with overlapping thunder and lightening. Sheets of rain ceaselessly pelted against the mountainsides and buildings of the Willey settlement. As the cliffs above began to crumble, the stream waters of the

Saco began to swell into the house. Explosions of trees and rocks permeated through the thunder, as the mountain gave up its grip and came down towards the little house. It was then that the family and farmhands left the sanctity of their home and scurried into the storm for safer grounds amidst the landslides and swirling floodwaters of the raging river.

The next morning, John Barker braved the flooded streams and rubble left by the storm and ventured to the Willey house. He was relieved to see wisps of smoke rising from the chimney. The yard was strewn with boulders as high as the abode itself. The shed was completely gone and the barn lay in shambles. Yet the house sat untouched. The walls of rock that had fled their stony perch, taking all in their path, had come to rest on both sides of the house. Not as much as a stone had scathed the structure.

He entered the house to find the smoldering embers, a circle of chairs with the Bible open on one of them, and a water line where the stream had rushed in through the door, stopping just short of the huddled seats. Yet not a soul was around. Totally exhausted, he fell asleep, but was later awoken by a low moaning sound. With no torch or lamp, he held still until morning.

The next morning, a search party arrived and released an ox that was trapped under the ruins of the barn—no doubt the source of the moaning. That was when the fate of the Willey settlement unfolded.

They found the remains of Polly Willey and one of her children under one of the great boulders near the front door. A few days later, one of the farmhands was found the same way. They buried them and made refuge for the cabin as the wild mountain night crept in.

The next day, the other farmhand and Sam Willey were found near the river's edge. Sally Willey, only five years old, was pulled from the Saco River the following Sunday. The three other children were never found. Were they forever sealed in a tomb of boulders and gravel? Were they washed downstream? Or did they, as some speculated, become crazy creatures of the wild mountains?

All in all, some thirty avalanches had taken place, leaving mile-long scars in the mountainside that are still visible to this day. The house stood dormant for eighteen years where passing travelers would pay homage to the tragedy. In 1844, it reopened as a hotel, then burned down during a storm in 1898. Its stone foundation is all that remains, clearly marked between a visitor's center and gift shop.

Could such a storm ever plague the present tenants of the notch again? Who knows? Maybe one hundred years from now tourists will be visiting three foundations and listening to another tale of curious New England.

The Willey House Memorial is in Crawford Notch in the White Mountain National Forest. Take Interstate Route 93 to Exit 35, Route 302. Follow for about twenty-five miles and the site is on the right in the notch of several mountains.

Dover

The Dover Mills

The Dover Mills still sits prestigiously at One Washington Center in the heart of Downtown Dover. The mill's history is ripe with tales of prosper and woe. That is why its walls are full of ghosts and otherworldly noises passing through the barrier of time that has long left them silent.

The mills go way back to the early days of the Industrial Revolution. John Williams and fellow investors formed the Dover Cotton Factory in 1812. They built their factory along the Cochecho River. Cochecho is an Abenaki Indian word for "the rapidly foaming water." The rapids produced great power for the early mill. In 1823, the name was changed to Dover Manufacturing Company as they were now manufacturing other items along with the cotton.

The haunted Dover Mill building where workers of the past still run their machines.

Mr. Williams was a fair boss for the times. He paid his worker girls forty-seven cents a day. They received room and board and put two cents per day towards medical.

Factory life was hard. The workers toiled for eleven to twelve hours a day. During the months of March to October, the workday ran from 6:30 a.m. to 6:30 p.m. with forty-five minutes for lunch.

John Williams moved to Boston around 1828, leaving James Curtis in charge of the mill. Curtis was harsh and insensitive to the woman workers there. He cut their wages from fifty-eight cents a day to fifty-three cents. He even imposed a fine of twelve and one half cents for any employee who showed up late. Conditions were dangerous in early mills. Many accidents left the workers scarred or maimed for life. Some were even killed by the unforgiving machines.

On December 30, 1828, the women had had enough. About four hundred of the eight hundred female workers stormed off the job and took up a picket line in front of the factory. This was the first strike by women in the workforce of the United States. Unfortunately, the strike was a failure. The owners of the mill put an ad out for replacements, and the women were forced to return to their jobs on January 1, 1829, with a reduction in pay.

The ever-expanding mill incorporated another name and began to manufacture clothes and other related goods. This branch was named the Cocheco Manufacturing Company. The spelling error in the name was due to an oversight by the state clerk when recording the birth of the business. Even the river now bears the name with the missing "H."

Years passed, and the mill grew into several buildings. One building of particular interest was new Building #1 that was built at the bend of the river known as "The Beach." This building was the site of the tragic fire that took place on January 26, 1907. The fire broke out on the fourth floor at about 6:30 p.m. Since the sprinkler system was down, the fire spread quickly. Workers had to leap from the windows, and many were injured. The firefighters fought the blaze for one and a half days in temperatures that reached twenty-six degrees below zero.

In the end, four people were lost to the fire, and the building was gutted. They rebuilt the structure, and by 1908, it was back in business. The million-dollar loss and the changing of the tides in manufacturing would soon prove too much for the giant mill complex.

In 1909, the factory was sold to Pacific Mills out of Lawrence, Massachusetts, and business resumed once again. At the end of World War I, things took a turn for the worst. Then came the depression, and the great mill finally closed its doors in 1937. In 1940, the town of Dover bought the mill at an auction. The town was the only bidder. The price of the complex was a mere $54,000.

They rented it to small businesses, but the buildings had fallen into a sad state of disrepair. By the 1960s, only the ghosts inhabited the empty shells that loomed over the center of town. In 1984, they

were given a new lease on life when Tim Pearson and Joseph Saw-
telle purchased the structures and renovated them to the present day
office and business facility that sits at One Washington Center. The
building lives once more with the advent of present day industry—and
yesterday's as well.

People standing outside of the building after every business is closed
have claimed to see strange glowing lights hovering around the upper
floor windows. Voices of the long dead seem to still echo through the
building, as if calling out over the clamor of the machinery that once
graced its inner walls. Or maybe it is the spirits of the past reliving that
tragic day of January, 1907. Other noises that are frequently heard are
the noises of old machinery. The sounds resemble old looms and other
manufacturing machines starting and stopping. Local historian Mark
Leno was told by a custodian who works the night shift that he has
heard the phantom machinery running at night while cleaning up. He
also stated that one of the towers is haunted. Ghostly voices and forms
have been witnessed in the tower. Other witnesses have seen eerie lights
emitting from the basement windows. This would not seem so strange,
but the basement has been securely sealed for many years.

Could the workers of the past still be drawn to their duties long after
their mortal time on earth? Is the machinery that maimed or claimed lives
also part of the spirit world, or is it just a byproduct of the ghost's never-
ending tenure at the haunted Cocheco Mill? Ask someone who presently
works there, or someone who used to, if you are brave enough.

Cocheco Mill is located at One Washington Center in Downtown
Dover, New Hampshire 03820. Take Interstate Route 95 to Route 16/
Spaulding Turnpike. Proceed about ten miles to Exit 8, Route 9 East.
Follow into center of town where mill is surrounded by Washington
Street, Central Avenue, and Main Street.

Ten Folsom Street

Do you believe in ghost trains? It seems that some residents of Dover
have a hard time *not* believing in them. At Ten Folsom Street, tenants of
a large apartment complex frequently experience the rattling and shaking of the building caused by, what appears to be, a train going by. This
would not be unusual about sixty years ago, but the train tracks next to
the building have not been in use for half a century. The paved-over rail
lines still play host to phantom trains which cause quite a commotion
around the building.

Folsom Street is a small street between Cushing Street and Belknap Street near the Cocheco River. The throughway runs over a set of old railroad tracks. Take Interstate Route 95 to Exit 5, Route 4 North. Bear onto Route 16 North. Take Exit 8, Route 9 (Silver Street) towards Dover Center. Bear left on Cushing Street, then right onto Folsom Street.

Bedard Haunting

This famous haunt is not very documented, as the residents of the home prefer to stay anonymous. I am including it for your perusal as it is a New Hampshire haunt. The brick home was built in 1939. This hardly competes in age with a colonial or historical home, but there has been plenty of time to store a ghost or two.

The occurrences include bizarre sounds of something scratching in the attic—and investigations proved they were not from an animal. Doors open and close on their own volition. The residents have also witnessed an elderly man in a wheelchair in one of the bedrooms. The most disturbing fact is that he has also been witnessed looking in the windows of the house from the outside, mainly the living room window. The identity of the specter is of question, as is the location of the home. Good luck.

Dublin

Fiddler's Choice Music Store

They say that the pleasing sounds of music is a gift from the heavens. It surprises me that more spirits who come back from beyond have not taken that idea to heart and soul when they embark on a haunting. This charming and irresistible music store is located in an antique farmhouse on Route 137 in Dublin. No one is saying too much about the history, but there are a few residual residents who might want to share their time with you—perhaps enjoy a song or two, as well. There are cold spots often felt in the store that move with the person who experiences them. The ghost of the store seems to like things a certain way, as furniture and musical instruments are often rearranged by unseen hands.

Owners and employees alike have experienced many occurrences that they call "playful poltergeist activity." The activity is nothing harmful, just interesting. Perhaps the phantoms of the music store are looking for attention and want to be heard. Maybe they should try music lessons. There is a lot of work out there for horror movie scores.

Fiddler's Choice Music Store is located on Route 137, less than one mile from the intersection of Route 101. Take Everett Turnpike to Exit 7, Route 101A. Follow Route 101A to Route 101 West. Follow Route 101 into Dublin, then bear right onto Route 137.

Durham

Three Chimneys Inn/ffrost Sawyer Tavern—
A Picture is Worth More Than a Thousand Words

Durham, New Hampshire is a quaint little town alive with the quintessence of what one might expect from the tranquility and beauty of the Granite State. The Three Chimneys Inn is no exception. The inn comes alive with guests mulling about and diners in the tavern filling the spirit of the fascinating antiquated structure with the sounds of the present. There are some from the past, though, who still make some noise of their own.

The house was built in 1649 by successful entrepreneur Valentine Hill. He and Thomas Beard were given the water rights to the Oyster River Falls. They set up a sawmill there that began Hill's legacy. He also owned a gristmill and 500 acres of what is now presently the Village of Durham.

Portions of the original homestead were actually carried up the Oyster River by gondolo, then assembled on the property. Gondolos were the characteristic carrier boats on the American rivers of that period. The house was typical for the times, with a single- room living quarters that acted as kitchen, living room, and bedroom. There was a basement also. Formerly used as a summer kitchen, the basement and outdoor fireplace is now known as the

The Three Chimneys Inn/ffrost Sawyer Tavern.

ffrost Sawyer Tavern. The house was sturdy enough to survive an Indian attack in 1694, while most of the nearby homes were destroyed by fire.

Nathaniel Hill, son of Valentine, made a few additions to the house starting with the expansion of the original structure both upwards and out-wards. Indian shutters were then added to repel flaming arrows. Years later, during the Revolutionary War, it became a storage facility for confiscated munitions taken from the British troops. In 1795, the barn was built and a cistern for water was put in. That same year, a piece of the property was deeded to the town for use as a burial ground. The historical graves still grace the area at the rear of the inn.

In the 1800s, George ffrost II purchased the property, then hired Jacob Odel (who is buried in the small cemetery next to the inn), to renovate the mansion to a more Federal style. The lower sloped roof and Italianate eaves and cupolas on both the house and barn that capture the allure of visitors, are the work of Mr. Odel. The ffrost family lived in the home for many years. The ffrost sisters built the lovely gardens on the grounds.

When James and Margaret Pepperell ffrost acquired the estate, they turned it into an elaborate summer home. In 1912, they added tennis courts, formal gardens, and a swimming pool.

It all went downhill from there. The mansion was sold and resold over the next several decades, until it lay in ruins. It was then purchased and renovated into the Three Chimneys Inn in 1998. The inn is presently listed in the National Register of Historical Places, as well as many registers of historical haunts.

Thomas B. Moriarty was caretaker and groundskeeper for the ffrost fam-ily during the years of 1952 to 1972 when they were away. Many strange things happened in the historic mansion. On many occasions, he witnessed the rocking chair in the living room sway to and fro with no visible being or any draft to initiate the movement. The chair is still there and witnesses still experience the creaking of the ghostly rocker. Many times he would ascend the stairs to the attic and bedroom, only to hear another set of footsteps from behind and feel the presence of someone else on the stairs with him.

Mr. Moriarty once witnessed the ghostly figure of a woman standing near the open hearth fireplace in the cellar that now houses the tavern. He is not the only recipient of the ghostly goings-on in the mansion. The executive chef of the tavern closed up at midnight as usual one night and returned to the basement to do his paperwork. Suddenly, he heard heavy footsteps clomping on the wooden floor above him. He was sure the inn was vacant, so he ran upstairs thinking it was an intruder or someone who may have been locked in by mistake. He called out as he searched the inn, but no one else was in the building save for himself. He shrugged off the experience and returned to his paperwork. A few minutes later, the foreboding footsteps returned. Once again, he exasperatingly searched the interior for a trespasser, but found he was alone in the public house. The incident would happen two more times that night, as the chef listened in apprehension to the phantom footsteps thump along the heavy wooden floorboards above.

Innkeeper Karen Meyer has had a few incidents of her own. Much of her time is spent upstairs in her office at her computer that is never turned off. One day, she left her workplace to greet a vendor in the tavern. They both headed up to her third floor office to complete a business transaction. When they got there, the door was locked. She was sure she hadn't locked the office, as she needed to return so quickly. The front desk manager, Merriane, had the only other key, but she was very busy at the time. Finally, the door was unlocked, and upon entering the room, another uncanny sight greeted the startled group. The computer was off.

Karen later tested the door and found that the door could not be locked unless the key was used to turn the bolt. Yet, her keys were locked inside the office.

Karen feels it was a good spirit or "angel on her shoulder" hinting for her to take a break. She had worked very hard before that warning, with little leisure time. She took the spirit's suggestion and went home.

Those involved with the house are not the only ones to witness the ghostly phenomenon. Many guests have also sensed a presence that follows them up the stairs.

Room six is where the ghost of Hannah Sawyer is said to materialize in front of guests. Hannah Sawyer was a young girl when she committed suicide in her bedroom—now guest room number six. Her picture hangs on the wall at the top of one of the stairways in the inn. Her apparition has also been seen peering through the railings of the stairs leading down to the ffrost Sawyer Tavern by patron and staff alike.

As Arlene, my wife, and I entered the Three Chimneys Inn, we were greeted by a desk clerk who was more than happy to show us the wonderful historic building. Arlene went right to work taking pictures while I absorbed the illustrious history present within the inn. I took some voice recordings, as well, but did not capture any spirits on tape. Then we came upon the picture of Hannah Sawyer. The young girl's portrait halted us in our tracks for two reasons. The first was that the look was almost surreal as she is shown peering up from a book with large dark eyes. The other was that the desk clerk bore an uncanny resemblance to the Sawyer girl in the very old depiction hanging over the stairway.

When we had the pictures developed, someone noticed that there was another transparent person in the photo. The body of a more modern woman in a white top and long skirt (located in the left lower corner of the photograph) is seen in the image. The angle of the shot was chosen to prevent reflection of the hallway off the glass, and no one was in front of the picture of Hannah Sawyer. There was also no one in the hallway. At such an angle as the photograph was taken, it would have to capture someone who would be in *front* of the picture during the shot. (We stood in the hall behind the portrait as to not be seen in the picture when it was taken.) How this photograph came to be remains one of the mysteries known only to the ghosts of the Three Chimneys Inn.

The Three Chimneys Inn/Sawyer ffrost Tavern is the oldest building in Durham. Who knows who else is still lurking among the twenty-three rooms of the inn? After visiting the delightful and picturesque house and grounds, why would they ever want to leave?

The inn and tavern are located at 17 Newmarket Road, Durham, New Hampshire 03824. 888-399-9777. E-mail: kmeyer@threechimneysinn. com. Take Interstate Route 95 to Exit 4, Spaulding Turnpike, Route 16/4 North into Newington. Follow to where Route 4 and 16 split. Route 4 is then called Piscataqua Road. Take Route 108, Dover Road South to New Market Street. Bear left onto Newmarket Street and the inn is immediately on your left.

Parking is in rear of the inn. The historical cemetery is behind the small wall along the edge of the parking lot.

Portrait of Hannah Sawyer with strange reflections.

Stairway to the ffrost Sawyer Tavern where the ghost of Hannah Sawyer is seen by employees and guests peering through the railing.

Smith Hall-University of New Hampshire

Colleges seem to always sport a ghost or two. I don't know if initiation pranks create legends, or if the old buildings they sometimes acquire come with prefab phantoms. This next ghostly tidbit falls into either scenario.

Smith Hall at University of New Hampshire is the oldest hall on campus. Although it holds only ninety-two residents, the cultural diversity of this building spans all walks of life, and apparently, one from the other side. The ghost is that of a mysterious woman who wanders the halls during the witching hours. She is said to pay visits to the unsuspecting residents of the hall. I spoke with the director of Smith Hall, and she said that she has not experienced the wandering wraith, although she recalled an old tale about a woman who committed suicide in the hall many, many years ago on the fourth floor. No one else in the hall has had a recent experience. It could be a product of urban legend or maybe the spirit has graduated to bigger things.

University of New Hampshire is located in Durham on College Road. Take Interstate Route 95 to Exit 5, Spaulding Turnpike, Route 16/4. Follow to split and veer onto Route 4, Piscataqua Road. Take Route 108 South to Mill Road. Take the left onto Mill Road, then right onto College Road.

The University is on your right.

The Trestle

While interviewing some of the locals and students of the University of New Hampshire, I came across a place where there really *is* another side of the tracks—in the spiritual world, anyway. It is an eerie place that runs along the Lamprey River on the Durham/Newmarket town border, aptly nicknamed "The Trestle." A few tales are told of why the site is so haunted.

A train once derailed at the bridge spilling cars onto the ground and into the river. One of the cars still sits in the river as a memorial to the tragic incident. People swimming in the river have been hurt, or have even met a worse fate while diving off the trestle and hitting the sunken boxcar. Needless to say, a lot of negative energy has been left behind in this area. The ghosts of those lost still permeate the air around the tracks and create a foreboding sense of fear.

In 1982, a man supposedly shot his wife and then turned the gun on himself at the trestle while his terrified children looked on. The local populace will either swear by it or give it a big *humbug*. Either way, it sounds like a place to be content to just read about.

     The trestle is accessible from Elm Street. Follow directions into Durham and follow Route 108 South to Elm Street. Bear right onto Elm Street and park where you can follow the tracks north. Pass over a small bridge, and a bit further up is the trestle. From what I was told, it is a small hike. The place is a hangout for locals. If you decide to trek into the trestle, do it at a reasonable time of day. Heed all common sense and stay out of the water and off the trestle. There need not be more ghostly or negative energy

East Kingston

Philbrick House

There are many accounts throughout history that tell of dormant ghosts. That is, they lie in peace until something unpleasant to their eternal rest rouses them. It is then that the ghosts, interrupted, become active. No one may ever find out why the said spirits have become restless. In the case of the Philbrick House, strong suspicion falls on the last will and testament of Eva Philbrick, who died in 1920. In her will, she clearly specified that the house must never be sold at auction or repossession. Perhaps this was a safety net to keep it in the family.

Obviously, one of the family never read the will, as the property was auctioned off in 1987 to Rick and Kerry Marshall. In 1988, they began renovations to the old house that began its life as a colonial cape in the 1830s. That is when the ghostly activity rose from the silent depths of the antiquated structure.

Inexplicable loud noises began to permeate the inner walls of the house. Lights would turn on in vacant rooms. Even the pans in the kitchen would begin rattling at all hours of the day and night. There was also a collection of antique clocks that began working on their own. Maybe she was trying to tell them it might be time to turn the place back to its original state. The residence is private so respect should be given.

The Philbrick House is located at 47 Depot Road (Route 107), East Kingston, New Hampshire 03827. Take Interstate Route 95 to Exit 1, Route 107 West. Follow into East Kingston. The house is just past the library on Route 107.

Eaton Center

Toll Hill

Someone once told me that animals cannot become ghosts because they supposedly do not have a soul. In all my years as a paranormal investigator, I have found that statement to be quite untrue. I have come across countless people who have sworn that they were visited by their recently deceased and beloved pets, or experienced the presence of an animal that was no longer of the living. Ghost dogs are illustrated throughout history as being omens of bad fate. Sightings are frequent of these phantom animals that also seem to cross the barrier of life and death.

Do you believe that animals can become spirits wandering eternally in search of resolution to their demise? Could they also still have some attachment to their masters and friends from beyond the grave? If so, then you are in good company. If not, then this next story just might make you a believer.

Toll Hill in Eaton Center is the scene of a tragic end for a horse that was caught in a blizzard. During the fierce storm, the loose horse sought refuge in an abandoned building on a farm. Unfortunately, the storm was so intense that drifts caused by the wind and snow covered and sealed the only opening for the horse to escape the structure. The cries of the horse were never heard. Attempts to break out of the building became futile as the panic-stricken horse tried to reunite with its master. The poor, tired horse died of exposure and starvation.

In the spring of 1925, the farmer found the lost horse's body in the building and remorsefully buried it somewhere on the farm. Shortly afterward people started seeing the ghost of a white horse trying to break out of the building. The farm has since been rebuilt and is now occupied by the living as well as the dead. Local residents know the parcel of land as "The Old Thurston Place." The ghost beast is seen endlessly trying to escape the house that became a deathtrap.

Maybe the owners should leave the door open for a while to let the spirit out. But then again, what else might enter?

Toll Hill is in Eaton Center just south of Conway. Take Interstate Route 93 to exit 32, Route 112. Route 112 is also known as the Kancamagus Highway. Follow into Conway. Take Route 153 South towards Eaton Center. Turn east onto Horse Leg Hill Road. About one and one-half miles down on left is the old farmhouse. It is now a private residence so please respect the owner's wishes.

Sunset Beach Woods—Home of Uncle Milt's Place

This was once a boy's camp, but before that, it was a small community. Now, it is an abandoned ghost town sporting numerous cellar holes and a few supernatural residents, as well. There once was a small cemetery where the residents of the area were buried. All the gravestones have been taken, for some reason, but one. One lonely stone sits marking what was once a burial ground. Old and worn, the marker sits as a lone icon for those who may have built the structures that formerly covered the quiet cellar holes.

Witnesses who have taken photographs of the single grave were astonished when the pictures revealed orbs and misty white figures hovering around the stone. It has been dubbed Uncle Milt's Place, probably in reference to the barely legible name on the stone. The brave souls who enter into the foreboding wood have another fright to contend with. It is reported that a demon dog roams the woods around the little village and will give chase when spotted.

Whether or not this is actually true is a matter of conjecture. Origins of the demon dogs trace back to Europe and have been known through the centuries as harbingers of ill omen. There are numerous reports of such animals throughout the United States. New England is host to several ghost dogs in Massachusetts, Rhode Island, Connecticut, and New Hampshire. Names like Moothe Doog, Black Striker, Black Shuck, and Snarly Yow are enough to make the bravest soul avert their eyes and retreat in haste. If you come across this particular demon dog, it is recommended that you do not run into the woods. It is said that the woods change and become unfamiliar. Even those who have trekked the forest have stated that they change mysteriously, and that the ill-fated hiker will become disoriented in what was, but a few moments before, familiar territory.

If this is not enough to make the squeamish evade this cursed ground, it is also reported that there are patches of quicksand around the area of the old village. With all of these possible supernatural and natural perils, it would appear that the smartest thing to do would be to read about this afflicted soil and be satisfied at that. There is very little information on the history of the location, or its former inhabitants, available. The fact that the town is abandoned, as witnessed by the old cellar holes and missing graveyard, makes a person wonder: What actually happened to the people, and where did their graves go?

Follow directions for above for Toll Hill. Further information can be obtained in Eaton Center.

Exeter

Lindenshire Mobile Home Park

Legend has it that a section of the trailer park was built on an old graveyard. Residents and visitors of the park have witnessed ghosts wandering lost within the eastern portion of the living commons. Other strange occurrences happen randomly within the trailers of that sector. Lights turn on and off. Doors open and close on their own and voices have been heard in areas where there are no humans present. The people of the community shun a section of woods called "Hobo Jungle" where they say glowing eyes watch them as they pass by the foreboding forest.

Legend, truth, products of a child's over active imagination, malfunctioning doors and electrical wiring, or angry spirits attempting to inform the residents that they may have illegally parked their mobile homes in the spirit world?

Lindenshire Mobile Home Park is located in lower Exeter off Linden Street. Take Interstate Route 95 to Exit 2, Route 101 West. Take Exit 12, Route 27/111 into Exeter. Follow Route 111 to Linden Street and bear left. The Exeter Cemetery will be on your right. The mobile home park is just past the cemetery over the river.

Francestown

Haunted Lake

In the mid-1700s, two men on route to Hillsborough stopped to camp by the lake. As the gibbous moon rose high in the night sky, so did the temper of one of the camping companions. Come morning, a sole sojourner packed his belongings and proceeded on his trek.

Not long after this weird night, residents passing the lake began to hear mysterious loud moans and shrieks permeating the disturbing hours of darkness. It was not until many years later that loggers unearthed a skeleton buried near the shore of the lake. The unfortunate being had obviously been victim to foul play. The other camper was never seen or heard from after that fateful night. Now, when the ominous moon rises over the haunted waters, residents on the lake must endure the moaning and shrieks that cry out for justice and peace.

Haunted Lake is located two miles east of Francestown on Route 136. Take Everett Turnpike/Route 293 to Exit 5, Route 114 in Manchester. Follow into Goffstown. Take Route 13 to Route 136. Follow Route 136 towards Francestown. Haunted Lake will be on left.

Franconia

Sugar Hill Inn

Ghosts and the White Mountains. It almost seemed inevitable. When you blend the White Mountains with harsh winters, landslides, Indian attacks, and the mountains with many ferocious animals, it becomes obvious that there will be a spirit or two lingering on the countryside. On the other hand, blend the beauty of the mountain scenery, the untainted air, the feel of nature at your door, and the complete lack of overcrowding, it becomes obvious why *spirits* would linger, as well.

The Sugar Hill Inn is the latter of the two. The Oakes family was one of the first settlers in Franconia in 1789. They built a farmhouse and planted their crops. The house was rather nice for a farmhouse. Post and beam construction, wide pine floors and trim were part of the charm that made guests feel welcome in the Oakes homestead. The floorboards were over two feet wide, in some cases, as there were plenty of tall trees to be had in the Northern New England area.

The house changed hands only one more time before a couple named Richardson purchased it in 1925. In 1929, they built a large addition onto the existing house, and opened up a hotel called the Caramat Inn. That same year, an Austrian born skier named Sig Buchmayr started America's first ski instruction school in Franconia. Although Beckett's-on-the-Hill sponsored the school, many people still needed lodging for the winter mountain fun that was beginning to flourish in the area.

Business boomed, and by the 1950s, Caramat Inn added three small cottages to accommodate the tourists. In 1972, the name was changed to the Sugar Hill Inn. Somewhere along the line, the addition of a few ghosts were made, as well.

An elderly couple came to visit the inn, then disappeared through a locked door as onlookers stood agape in alarm of the occurrence. They may have been regulars of the inn coming to a place that they loved for one final hurrah. The silhouette of a male figure is seen in the kitchen where the original owner of the house, Mr. Oakes, passed away.

The ghosts of the inn are not bothersome. They just want to enjoy the hospitality at Sugar Hill that has made the hostel second to none. The seven-room main house and six-room cabins have breathtaking views of the Presidential Range. Some even have fireplaces to warm the chill of the mountain air. New owners Judy and Orlo Coots go out of their way to make sure guests feel at home at the Sugar Hill even if the guests are the type that pass through walls on their way out.

The Sugar Hill Inn is located on Route 117, P. O. Box 954 in Franconia, New Hampshire 03580. 603-823-5621. Take Interstate Route 93 to Exit 38. Take a left at the stop sign. Bear right onto Route 18 into Franconia. Bear left onto Route 117, and the inn is one half mile up hill on right.

The Coppermine Trail

Throughout history, the settlers of the "New World" have scoffed at the powers of the Native Indians' deities. Their scorn has always resulted in tragic tales of wrath and revenge. The spirits of the American Indian are eternally rooted in this great land, watching over and protecting their people. Though just and fair, in a moments notice, they can summon all the powers of nature and beyond upon their transgressors.

In New England, there are countless tales of such wrath upon the early pioneers who encroached upon sacred Indian soil without regard of consequence. One of the most tragic tales of revenge still echoes through the White Mountains to this day. There was once a town, but it lives no more.

The year is sometime about 1850 when settlers came to the Franconia Notch area and discovered copper. The discovery was a boom for the region, and immediately a mining company set their sights on the vein of copper and a town.

They laid tracks to the vein and began to build a town, but something was wrong. Old records show that in the building of this little community, they were beset with eerie hindrances that defied all natural logic. Every time a house was finished, it would be minus the roof come first light. Foundations excavated the previous day were found filled in as if there was never a pebble tossed asunder. Even the construction equipment was plagued with supernatural forces that obstructed the erecting of the town.

As the conditions worsened, the people began to notice Indians sneaking around in the woods carefully monitoring their progress of the town. One day the pastor of the town asked a native what was going on, and he came forth to tell him that they were building on sacred Indian burial land where many braves and chiefs rested. The Great Spirits were warning them of this fact. He was sent to petition that they move the town a few hundred yards away, lest a most tragic fate befall them.

It seems progress had no regard for the infinite power of the Great Ones, and the town was completed in haste and ignorance of the Indians' pleas. Two hundred men, women, and children settled into the thriving community. Most of the men worked in the copper mine while the children attended the school. There was a store, blacksmith shop, and two churches. It seemed odd that the churches were never subject to the unearthly visitors of the night. The Indians, however, made it clear that the Great Spirits did not want to impede upon their sacred place as a sign of mutual respect and that the settlers should do the same and move.

This sounded too much like a fairy tale for the community to comprehend and business went on as usual. The Indians slowly disappeared, and it seemed the townspeople had won their battle—or had they?

It was a hot day in August of 1859, and the town was going about its usual business when, what witnesses in the notch and ancient Indian record reveal, the sky turned to a bloody red over the area of the village and a great thunder shook the earth. Witnesses from afar watched as a dark cloud formed into what resembled a great hand and plunged upon the notch where the copper mine sat. The next instance, all was quiet and the sky was once again blue and still.

No one was prepared for what they would observe when they reached the small town. Not only had the mine collapsed, killing every worker inside, but the town was completely void of every living creature. Smoke wisped in the fireplaces and tables had half consumed plates of food, yet not a soul was ever found from the village. Everything appeared as if they'd vanished into thin air. The only building that was left unscathed was the church of the pastor who had pleaded with the townsfolk on behalf of the Natives.

The mining company wanted to reopen the mine, but there was not an individual brave enough to mock the Great Spirits this time, and so the buildings of the little community sat and crumbled with time. The cellar holes and fragments of what was once a thriving village now sit among the burial mounds of the great chiefs and warriors that, even in death, were intruded upon by the White Man and his progress—but not for long.

If you should wander down the Coppermine Trail, remember it is permitted to visit, but I would not advise settling in for any length of time.

The Coppermine Trail is located off Route 116 in Franconia. Take Interstate Route 93 to Exit 32, Route 112, Lincoln/ Woodstock. Stay straight on Route 112 at the intersection of Route 3. Follow Route 112 to Route 116 and bear right onto Route 116. Trailhead for the Coppermine Trail will be on right.

Gilford

Kimball Castle

A castle in New England? Next you are going to say, "It is haunted!" You bet. There are several castles strewn across the landscape of New England. All of them house mysterious visitors from the afterlife that either lived in the great abodes or came with the furnishings. Kimball Castle is no exception.

The castle was built in 1897 for railroad magnate Benjamin Ames Kimball and his family. After a trip to Germany, Mr. Kimball was awestruck by the great palaces along the Rhine River. He chose Locke's Hill in Gilford to construct an exact replica of one of the German fortresses.

An English architect designed the woodwork and ironworks for the castle, then had it shipped to Boston. It was then transported by Kimball's railcars to Gilford. A giant three-inch thick oaken door led into the main foyer. Wrought iron lanterns, gargoyles, and even carved doorknockers were employed as functional ornamentations to the castle. It truly was, and still is, a sight to behold. The Kimball family lived in their summer castle from early spring to late fall.

Benjamin Kimble passed away in July of 1920 at age eighty-six. Sadly, his wife had died earlier, as had his son, Henry, in 1919. Henry's wife, Charlotte Atkinson Kimble, was now sole possessor of the estate. Although she lived in the castle until her death in July of 1960, she despised the dark, dank, and drafty abode. She also feared it might fall into ill will. Between 1957 and 1959, she willed the property to the Mary Mitchell Humane Society and the Alvord Wildlife Sanctuary. She also willed a hefty sum of money for the upkeep of the acreage. This money somehow disappeared, and even worse, the land and castle were totally neglected and fell into disrepair.

The society wanted to subdivide the land and sell it, but the will was ironclad. After many years of abandonment, the castle was given to the town. It stood again dormant until the 1990s, when a pair of investors proposed a resort for the once great citadel. This fell through, and the years took its toll on the land. Vandals took everything, from the great tapestries that adorned the walls to the gargoyles that stood sentinel at each corner of the castle. Even the beautiful stained glass windows were now in slivers, strewn along the grounds surrounding the crumbling relic.

Haunted Kimball Castle overlooking Lake Winnipesaukee.

The ghosts are, for the most part, the only permanent residents left in the bastion these days. Witnesses have reported a strong presence in the main part of the castle. The spirit of a woman is commonly seen near the sink in the old carriage house. One caretaker would open the heavy oak door to let light into the castle. When he turned for but a moment, the door would slam shut. Being of great magnitude, the door would take more than an average breeze to even make it creak, let alone close completely.

Mrs. Kimball's sewing room is another place of strange occurrence. The room has vistas from all sides with large windows where the most sunlight could be immersed into the chamber for fine handy work. This room was equipped with electric lighting, but that has long since been shut off. Lights still seem to turn on and then after a while extinguish themselves as if someone had entered to embark on a task, then finished and left.

Items were known to vanish from where they were placed, only to reappear in another location. Books fly off the shelves and plants even take on wings as they sail across the vast rooms of the castle. Family members attested to a hazy form that is seen entering and leaving the castle.

At present, the estate seems occupied. When I inquired about the castle, it was for sale. On our visit, however, the carriage house living quarters had been rebuilt and the people there seem to be renovating the castle. Permission should be obtained before roaming the castle grounds. The residents there might even give you a tour. Pay a visit to Kimball Castle and experience the Rhine in New England. Maybe you can own a piece of haunted New Hampshire if it is still for sale. The ghosts would really appreciate seeing the castle brought back to its original splendor.

The castle is located on Lockes Hill Road in Gilford, New Hampshire 03249. Take Interstate Route 93 to Exit 20, Route 11 East. Travel past the town of Laconia into Gilford. Take a right onto Lockes Hill Road. There are great views of the castle from Lockes Hill Road. Seek permission from the home at top of hill before possibly trespassing on someone's property.

One of the massive oaken doors of the haunted castle.

Goffstown

Goffstown Historical Society

Haunted historical societies are great research tools because the information needed is right there in your face when you enter the building. They are always born of some historical building that was donated for the continual preservation of history, and apparently haunts, as well. Goffstown Historical Society is no exception. It started its life as a general store built by William Parker in 1804. Upon his death in 1839, the business went to his two sons, John M. and David A. Parker. They continued the store until 1872, when they moved their business to Main Street in Goffstown. The Parker brother's store remained in business until the 1960s. The original building was used for storage and housing for the store workers and loggers.

Descendant, Mrs. John E. Parker, then turned it into a clubhouse for her literary and social group. It also served as a function facility for the town. By the mid 1960s, the building's upkeep became too much for the small guild and reverted back to the Parker family. It was then that John E. Parker donated the structure to the historical society. In 1974 the building was dedicated as the Goffstown Historical Society and is now on the well-known National Register of Historic Places. It is also in the lesser but more intriguing national register of haunted places.

It is said that John Parker haunts the building. While he was alive, he was known to walk around the rooms and chant while turning the lights on and off. During renovations, Parker's grandson was staying in a cottage behind the old building. In the dead of night, he would witness the lights go on and off at random and hear a faint chanting sound coming from within the building. Some witnesses have seen the silhouette of a man at the second floor windows long after the society has been locked up for the night. The current residents of the old Parker tavern across the street have observed the ghostly phenomena for years. The police have been called on occasion, but always fail to find any living entity in the building.

Eleanor Porritt has been Volunteer Curator of the society and museum for twenty years. She has not been in the building in the dead of night when the activity seems to come to life, but has talked to the woman in the house across the street about the ghostly occurrences. She related to me how students of St. Anselm's College in Goffstown came in one night and performed a paranormal investigation in the society building. Unfortunately they never divulged the results to her.

Former president of the Society, Andrea Card told me that although she has not had any contact with the ghost, Bruce Knox, who was hired to build an addition, had a few meetings with the inquisitive spirit. The ghost actually communicated to the contractor on a few occasions about how well the addition to the building looked.

If you go to the Goffstown Historical Society website, they mention that the building is reportedly haunted, and encourage visitors to come to find out for themselves. Now that's a society striving to preserve every aspect of the past—including the people themselves.

The Goffstown Historical Society is located two miles out of Goffstown Center on 18 Parker Station Road, Goffstown, New Hampshire 03045-3312.

Take Everett Turnpike to Exit 5, Route 114 West towards Goffstown/ Henniker. Bear left onto Mast Road/Route 114 West. Follow Route 114 West at split. Bear left onto NH 114/ N. Mast Street. Take a right onto Parker Station Road.

Saint Anselm's College

The Alumni Hall at this college is haunted by a monk who reportedly committed suicide by jumping from the fourth floor window. He is now eternally bound to wander the place of his transgression. Witnesses have seen the ghostly monk floating through the fourth floor hallways as lights begin to flicker with his passing.

Saint Anselm's College is located at St. Anselm's Road, Goffstown, New Hampshire 03045. Take the Everett Turnpike to Exit 5, Granite Street. Go west on Granite Street to Main Street. Take a left onto Main Street and then a right onto Varney Street. Bear right onto Mast Road, then left onto College Avenue. Once in Goffstown, this becomes St. Anselm's Drive.

Hampton

Jonathon Moulton House

The old Moulton House is a historical landmark hidden among the trees where the Route 1 North exit ramp connects with Route 101. This most unsuspecting building houses one of the most famous legends of all New Hampshire. It is a legend that seems to have several chapters, yet no ending to date. Many a campfire has flickered in the petrified faces of those who have heard the narrations of General Jonathon Moulton's deeds in life, and how his home still serves him and his wife long after their deaths. If you are curious as to what keeps the General and his wife from eternal rest, then by all means stoke the fire or turn the wick in your lamp up a notch, and lets begin the tale of the man who dealt with the devil.

Jonathon Moulton was born in Hampton, New Hampshire on July 22, 1726. In his youth, he was an apprentice to a cabinetmaker, but was able to buy his freedom in 1745 at age nineteen. In that year, he married Abigail Smith and set out on some very successful business ventures. The couple had eleven children, so a large home was inevitable. As the years went on, he served as Captain in the French and Indian Wars. He also served as a representative for the New Hampshire Legislature. Many of the time would say that Mr. Moulton was quite a ruthless businessman. They obviously liked him enough to keep electing him as representative, though.

In 1763, he was given land that once belonged to the now extinct Ossipee Indian Tribe. The land is located on the shore of Lake Winnipesaukee. With this land, he formed Moultonborough, Sandwich, Tamworth, Center Harbor, New Hampton, and Moultonville.

Moulton amassed quite a fortune in little time. His lavish ornate mansion was evidence of his wealth. It is said that his wealth was due to a pact he had made with the devil. It is claimed that Jonathon Moulton sold his soul to the devil for two boots full of gold each month. He was told to leave a pair of boots in front of the fireplace on a certain day of the month, and when he arose in the morning, they would be filled with the precious ore. This he did, and the devil stayed true to the deal. Old Moulton revered himself as a sharp dealer in business. It would seem that he thought he could con the curiosity out of a cat. When the devil went to fill his boots on the Ides of March in 1769, he found that no matter how much he put in, the leathers would not load up. Satan pulled one of the boots from the hearth and found that not only was the sole cut out, they were placed over holes cut in the floor so that the gold streamed into the cellar. The irate Lucifer immediately flew into a hellish rage and burned the house to the ground.

The General Jonathon Moulton Home.

The now humbled Captain built a more modest home in place of the first. Soon after, he became Colonel of the Third Regiment in the Revolutionary War. On September 21, 1775, Abigail Moulton died of small pox and was buried in the garden by the house. It was said that she swore to him that she would come back and haunt him if he remarried while she was still being mourned.

Evidently, the Colonel was neither superstitious or one for wasting time as he married Sarah Emery within a year of his wife's death. He reportedly even stripped his dead wife of her burial jewelry before she went into the ground and gave it to his new wife as a gift of love. Not long after the newlyweds settled into the house did Abigail keep her promise.

One night, as the couple dined, an unseen entity pulled the rings from Sarah's fingers and the jewels from her neck. They were never seen again. Abigail thought nothing of waking the weary couple in the night with doors closing and shadows moving about the house. The colonel could not be too bothered by the events, as he left for war again leading his now Second Regiment at the Battle of Saratoga in 1777. Soon, the war was over and the Post-War Depression left the Colonel broke. Some say it was Abigail's revenge on him for breaking his promise years before.

Things began to look better for Moulton. On March 25, 1785, he became Brigadier General of the First Regiment. The honor only lasted a few years as the general died suddenly on September 18, 1787, aged sixty-one years, one month, and twenty six days. He had four more children with Sarah in the time of their marriage, as well. Though he was buried beside Abigail in the garden, this did not stop Abigail from haunting the house that Sarah still resided in.

Slaves and the widowed wife frequently witnessed the ghost of Abigail wandering the halls of the home trying to reclaim it as her refuge in life and death. The Whipple family later bought the estate and actually performed an exorcism to rid the incommodious Abigail from the home. It worked, but only for a while.

Soon, the railroads came, and workers stayed at the house while laying tracks near the building. Somewhere along the line, the remains of Jonathon Moulton and his wife were covered by the tracks and completely lost. In the 1850s, the house was moved to its present location at the corner of Route 1 and Drakeside Road, forever misplacing the whereabouts of the couple's graves. A marker was placed in the Pine Grove Cemetery as a memorial to General Moulton. It is on the left side of the graveyard near the rear as you enter through its gates. There is no marker for his wife, however. Maybe this is one reason why she is still angry.

As time rambled on, the estate fell into disrepair, yet people still feared the haunted house and would not venture inside its walls. Abigail's ghost still wreaked havoc within the home even after it was moved. Around 1900, it was purchased and restored as a private residence. Today, it serves as an insurance office, yet the spirit of Abigail still roams the grounds, perhaps looking for the same eternal recognition the general was given—a memorial stone.

Did General Jonathon Moulton really dance with the devil for the precious ore that was bestowed upon him each month? Was he really devious in stripping the jewelry from his first wife before her burial? Perhaps when it is your time, you can ask him—depending on which way you might be going, of course.

> The Moulton House is now a private residence and not open for guests or tours. It can be seen at the corner of Route 1 North and Drakeside Road. Take Interstate Route 95 to Exit 2, Route 101 East towards Hampton. Take the Lafayette Road exit and turn around somewhere on Lafayette Road. Get onto Route 1 North, and the home is on your right. Caution is advised; this is an entrance ramp to Route 1 and is very busy, so do not stop on the road.

Eunice Cole's Local Haunts

Almost everybody is well acquainted with the Salem witch trials of 1692. Although they are the most publicized in American history, they certainly were not the first. Other colonies had their own dealings with witches and warlocks making deals with the devil. New England is besieged with historical accounts of these minions of the dark side, flying on brooms and casting the *evil eye* on any undertaker who fell into their disfavor. Even New Hampshire can boast about the perils of witchery—at least one, anyway. Eunice Cole was the only person in New Hampshire to be accused and jailed for witchcraft.

Maybe that is why she haunts the Tuck Museum, once residence of Frank Fogg, and the Founder's Park across the street. Or maybe it is the nature of how she was crudely buried with a stake supposedly driven through her heart. Maybe it is because the museum and park are presently located where her cottage once stood. Could it be all three reasons? Put your ghost detecting skills to work as you read on about Hampton's solitary seer of sorcery.

Eunice Cole came to America on February 20, 1637, with her husband, William. Little else is known except that her husband was sixty-three years old at the time of their arrival. *When* Eunice was born, and where, seem to remain a mystery to this very day. They were granted land in present Quincy, Massachusetts, but did not stay long. The couple followed Reverend John Wheelwright to New Hampshire in November of 1637. There he bought land from the Indians and founded the town of Exeter. William Cole was one of the signers of the deed for the land. In 1640, they moved to Hampton where they decided to settle for good. Why they left Exeter is anybody's guess, or maybe it will become clearer as the story unfolds.

Although they had forty acres of land in Hampton, they were still considered poor. Goodwife Cole, as she was known, was a bit too outspoken for her time. Goodwife or "goody" is a polite term given to the lower class married women of the period. Between 1645 and 1656, she appeared in court several times for her vile tongue about the community. As expected, "goody" Cole went a bit too far. It is alleged that she cursed a group of sailors who thought it fun to goad the old woman before they set sail by saying that they would never see home again. Upon return, a storm whipped up and wrecked the ship as it passed the Isle of Shoals. Those who had overheard the venomous words of Eunice Cole felt convinced that she was responsible for the deed.

She was arrested for witchcraft in 1657, and spent the next several years in a Boston prison. She was released in 1660 to care for her older and ailing husband. Within a year, she was back in jail on the same charge.

William Cole died on May 26, 1662. Eunice was released shortly after, but found no land to go home to. The town had sold it to pay for the care of her husband and her imprisonment. She then laid a curse on the townspeople, and was, as the crow flies, led directly back to the hoosegow. By 1671, she was back in Hampton, a poor old woman. The charitable townsfolk built a small cottage and reluctantly took turns caring for her—probably out of fear of being cursed again or having to pay for her imprisonment out of their pockets. Either way, she lived the rest of her life in the small shack that was given to her. This is where the Tuck Museum and Founder's Park sits today.

Some lessons are learned hard, if ever. She found herself in trouble a few more times, and spent short stints in jail again between 1671 and her death in 1680. When she passed away, the neighbors dragged her body outside and pushed it into a shallow grave. Before they put her in her final resting spot, they drove a wooden stake through her heart as an attempt to finally exorcise the demons that resided within her in life and to keep her in the grave. No one knows where she was actually buried, but it is taken as fact that her unmarked grave is in close vicinity of the Tuck Museum. The stake was not as effective as the citizens had hoped it would be, however. Her spirit has been seen roaming the area for many years.

The Tuck Museum placed an unmarked stone on the lawn as a memorial to Eunice Cole in 1963. It is quite uncanny how the stone, when looked at from the park, resembles the crooked face of an old woman. The shadow that cast upon the snow as we photographed it made us jump back a bit and take heed. Could this be the likeness of Eunice Cole? Those who have witnessed her ghost might think so.

The Tuck Museum was once the Fogg homestead, where the Fogg family reported seeing the ghost of Eunice Cole on several occasions in and around the house. The Tuck Museum has had its share of strange occurrences such as footsteps in empty rooms and doors opening and closing. Shadows are no stranger to the interior of the museum. Especially when the dark silhouette resembles a feeble old woman.

The park across the street is surrounded by stones with plaques of the founding families of Hampton. On the far side of the green is the stone that reads "Cole 1640". She is said to haunt the green as well. Perhaps that is her final resting area, and she is looking for more restitution than was given her in 1938, when a committee made copies of the court documents accusing her of witchcraft and burned them. They then put them in an urn for burial. The urn was never buried and still sits in the museum for all to see. Perhaps to prevent future run-ins with ghost "goody" Cole, the past should be buried.

Eunice Cole Memorial Boulder. Note how it resembles the face of an old woman with some sort of hat or scarf.

Tuck Museum where Eunice Cole's shack once stood.

Follow directions for Moulton Home onto Lafayette Road. Take the first right onto Park Avenue. Museum and Founder's Park will be on both sides of the road about one-third of a mile on Park Avenue.

Founder's Park across from Tuck Museum where the ghost of Eunice Cole is reported to roam.

Pine Grove Cemetery

The reason this cemetery is included in the Hampton chapter is not that it might be haunted, but because of *who* is buried there. The seemingly unassuming Pine Grove Cemetery sits on the side of Route 101E, curbed on both ends by homes.

The burial ground was established in 1654 and is among the oldest cemeteries in Hampton. But it is not only who might be buried there that is of particular interest, but who is *not* interred in the grounds as well.

One of the most famous ghosts of Hampton, if not all of New Hampshire, is Valentine Marston. Val Marston was born February 14, 1879, and was eleven years old when he died on October 12, 1890. He was playing with one of his father's old guns in his yard when the relic exploded, severely wounding him. The wounds themselves were not a peril, but in those days, lead poisoning was. He succumbed to the wounds due to poisoning. Since then, his ghost has been seen countless times by townspeople and tourists.

One family was walking the beach during vacation and spotted the little boy dressed in a sailor suit and cap, standing in front of a white house. They knew he was not of this world by the way he glowed, even in the morning light. When the father meandered towards him to see if he was real, he disappeared.

The house he lived in is, or was, haunted. It stood on Lafayette Road, but was moved to Woodland Road back in the 1980s. The present owners state that they have not experienced anything out of the ordinary, but previous owners have had to share the home with the phantom youngster. The ghost of Val is a pleasant one and not harmful. He has appeared to many of the owners including the Clement family and the Sanborn's. He has even appeared at the back door presenting flowers, only to vanish when Mrs. Sanborn reached out to take them.

His spirit is seen about the area according to many witnesses who have come in contact with the misty boy in the sailor suit. If he is so prone to wander, it might be noted that the curious can visit Pine Grove Cemetery where a number of the Marston family is buried. There you will see a large, rough stone on top another rocky base. The inscriptions are simple. One side reads, "Marston Died 1890".

There is, among the interred, one stone that is but a mere memorial to a lost hero. He was not lost in battle or at sea, but his own backyard. The stone is for General Jonathon Moulton, who is another famous Hamptonite both during his acclaimed life and hundreds of years after his death. Jonathon Greeenleaf Whittier penned a great poem of the life and death of Jonathon Moulton. Whittier wrote many accounts of New England that are a must read for the enthusiast of New England legend and folklore. The general and his wife, Abigail, were buried in the garden of their Hampton estate. Abby died in 1774 and the general in 1787. After that, the railroads came through and the house was moved to a new location, forever displacing the exact placement of the graves.

In a sort of repentance for the oversight by the citizens of Hampton, the memorial stone was erected in his honor among the other Moulton stones in the cemetery. Does he now haunt the graveyard? It is not likely that the general even knows about his petite monument. If anyone would have reason to haunt the area, it would be his wife, Abigail, who received no stone or mention for her plight of being lost. They might find that haunting the cemetery may possibly allow them more recognition. All being said, the venture to the historical burying ground is a must while in Hampton. Historical cemeteries are, if not haunted, at least full of Yankee spirit.

Follow directions to the Tuck Museum and go past museum to the intersection of Park Avenue and Route 101E. Bear left onto Route 101E and Pine Grove Cemetery will be almost immediately on the left.

Entrance to Pine Grove Cemetery.

General Moulton Memorial erected in his honor.

Marston Monument.

Hanover

Dartmouth College-Alpha Theta

A wretched incident on this particular piece of property has left paranormal repercussions that now span decades. Many years ago, the boiler in the Alpha Theta house exploded, burning the building to its foundation. Unfortunately, some of the frat brothers and their female companions were victims of the horrible event.

A new house was built on the old foundation, but some of the original inhabitants still remain in the building. Specters are frequently seen, and many have felt the presence of an unseen entity in the rooms about the fraternity. The most active area of the house seems to be in and around the basement that is the only original part of the previous structure.

Dartmouth College is the ninth oldest institution of higher education in the United States. It was named after William Legge, the 2nd Earl of Dartmouth. Eleazer Wheelock, a Congregational Minister from Connecticut, founded the school in 1769, after New Hampshire Governor John Wentworth gave him some land to form such a school. A charter from King George III created the college "for the education and instruction of the youth of the Indian tribes of this land…and also of English youth and any others." This inclusion in the charter probably had something to do with the fact that Samson Occum, a Mohegan Indian, was not only one of Wheelock's first students, but played a major role in the creation of the college. The wording is strange for our time, but don't forget they did not have erasers back then. Once set in ink, forever in ink.

Dartmouth College is located in Western Central New Hampshire. Take Interstate Route 93 to Route 89 North. Take Exit 18, Route 120 in Lebanon. Bear right at the end of the exit and follow 4.1 miles to a fork. Bear right at the fork. Follow the road to East Wheelock Street. Turn left onto East Wheelock Street for two-tenths of a mile.

Hart's Location

Notchland Inn

According to the 1992 State Census, the population of Hart's Location, New Hampshire boasted a whopping forty people. With no post office, town hall, police department, church, or fire department, it is by far the smallest town in New Hampshire. If they had counted its resident ghost, it would have pushed the populace up to forty-one.

The resident ghost resides at the beautiful Notchland Inn. The Notchland was originally a mansion built in 1862 by Sam Bemis. It sits on one hundred acres of land with a surrounding view of the White Mountains. In 1900, Florence Morey acquired the estate and turned it into a boarding house. Having become bored with that notion, it then became a hotel called the "Inn Unique." It has been a place of lodging for visitors to the mountains ever since.

The thirteen lavishly spacious guest rooms have their own fireplaces and private baths. The amenities and scenic vistas are enough to make a person want to stay forever. It seems that someone has.

Ed Butler, owner and innkeeper, related to me that several guests have felt the mysterious presence of a spirit in the inn. One couple even claimed that a ghost named "Abigail" wrote her name on the mirror in their room. This kind of surprised Ed, for he remembered when he was cleaning the attic and discovered an antiquated scripture. It was a letter from a mother to her daughter, and the name on the paper was none other than Abigail. Abigail Jones to be exact. It has been assumed that since none of the owners ever had an Abigail in the family, that this person may have been a servant of the Bemis family.

If you do not experience the spirit of Abigail, what might *seem* a bit less thrilling is still as rich with history and adventure at the Notchland. There is a tombstone that sits ominously in the living room. It is the stone marker of Nancy Barton who died in 1778 at the edge of the property while pursuing her disloyal betrothed. It seems the ruthless man wooed the unsuspecting woman, then stole away one night with her fortune. When Nancy realized she had been swindled out of her dowry, she set out in a fierce storm to catch the crooked scoundrel. Unfortunately, the storm proved too much for the girl and she was overcome by exposure and died near a brook and a pond that now bears her name.

On the stone reads the inscription, "NANCY, WHO DIED IN PURSUIT OF HER FAITHLESS LOVER". There is a path that leads to the original grave. Her resting place is now marked with a cairn. (A cairn is a pile of stones used to mark a grave. This custom can be traced as far back as the

Iberian-Celtic people and the Norse tribes that roamed this land many years before the European explorations.)

The charm and adventure of the inn and surrounding area is a must for visitors of the White Mountains. If you are there and feel a peculiar tingle of another presence, or wake up to an autograph on the mirror, just remember that it is a warm welcome from the personnel of the inn that you cannot see. Hart's Location may be the smallest settlement in the state, but it does have at least one ghost, which might be more than most other places can boast.

The Notchland Inn is located on Route 302, Hart's Location, New Hampshire 03812. 800-866-6131. Take Interstate Route 93 to Exit 40, Route 302 towards Twin Mountain. Follow Route 302 past Twin Mountain into Hart's Location. The Notchland is located on Route 302.

Henniker

The Legend of Ocean Born Mary

It is true that legends endure the span of time much longer than factual accounts. They are much more dazzling in narrative and can be added to without the consequence of blotting the annals of true history. Legends, however, are born of that truth that lies in the archives of the past and will always be subject to embellishment. This is where truth and tale cross. When this happens, we must hold in our hearts what we believe is the truth in order to keep the romance of a story alive. Such is the case of Ocean Born Mary.

The year is 1720. It is July 28th and the bow of the *Wolf* is pointed straight towards Boston Harbor. The ship is filled with Scottish-Irish immigrants headed towards Colonial America from Londonderry, Ireland to settle in Londonderry, New Hampshire on a land claim given to them by the Throne of Britain.

Off the portside of the vessel is another ship flying the flag of a privateer, or pirate, as we know them throughout history. The pirate ship bears down swiftly upon the *Wolf* and is boarded by a band of looters led by the ruthless, yet handsome, Don Pedro. As his men begin to loot and gather the passengers together, he hears a cry from down below.

He halts his men and saunters into the hold with cutlass in hand only to find Elizabeth Fulton and her husband, James, tending to a newborn baby. As she holds the baby protectively in her arms, the pirate sheaths his cutlass and asks, "What is the baby's name?"

"She hasn't one yet." The mother replies.

Don Pedro becomes quite overcome by the little new born baby and speaks with a more amorous tone. "If you would be so kind as to name the baby Mary, after my mother, then I shall see that everybody onboard this ship is returned their goods and left unharmed."

"That we shall do," says the mother.

The fearsome pirate exits the hold and returns a few moments later with a beautiful piece of green brocaded silk from the Orient. "This is for Mary." He says. "Use it for her wedding dress."

The *Wolf* made port in Boston and, unfortunately, James Fulton died shortly after.

Mrs. Fulton took Mary and moved to Londonderry as planned, where Mary grew up to be a tall beautiful red-headed young woman. In 1742, Mary married James Wallace and, as requested, did wear a gown made from the silk that Don Pedro had given her parents years before. Remnants of the famous dress are on display to this day at the New Hampshire Historical Society in Concord and at the libraries of Henniker and Londonderry.

The couple had five children, four boys and one girl. Legend has it that James Wallace died young and left Mary a widow in care of all five children. In the meantime, Don Pedro had given up his pirate life and rowed up the Contoocook River to a parcel of land where his ship carpenters built a beautiful home for him. Much of the home itself resembled his trusty pirate ship. As it turns out, Don Pedro was actually an English nobleman who was given six thousand acres of land by the King of England, but preferred the exciting and dangerous life as a swashbuckler on the high seas. Now still young and prosperous, he settled on his vast tract of territory that later became present-day Henniker, New Hampshire.

News of Mary's plight reached the ears of the former buccaneer. He beseeched that she come live with him and that he would care for her and her children. Some say she married the man, and there are others who swear that Don Pedro had given up piracy earlier and changed his name to James Wallace, then married Mary. No matter what the turn of events, Mary lived in the home of Don Pedro and cared for him.

One night, a few old friends of Don Pedro paid them a visit. There was much conversation, and Mary paid no heed to the unruly guests. All of a sudden, she heard a shout and then the voice of Don Pedro cursing the other men. Mary went out back where she saw Don Pedro lying in the yard with a cutlass still in him. She removed the sword, and before he died, he told her where he had hidden all the gold and jewels he had amassed from his earlier profession. He also requested that she bury him under the hearth of the fireplace so he could always be there to look out for her. She did as he wanted and lived the rest of her life in the house. She was ninety-four years old when she died on February 15, 1814. She is presently buried in the Williams lot in Henniker's Centre Cemetery behind the town hall now called The Community Building. The stone is adorned with the traditional weeping willow and urn that were popular for that period. The inscription reads, "IN MEMORY OF WIDOW MARY WALLACE WHO DIED FEB. 15 A.D. 1814 IN THE 94TH YEAR OF HER AGE". Her grave is easy to spot twelve rows back with a special plaque in front of it that reads, "OCEAN BORN MARY."

The story does not end there. Her spirit remained in the house after her death. Many people claimed to have seen a tall red-headed woman in the windows of the old house when it was unoccupied. People claim that they have seen her ghost in a spectral horse- drawn carriage moving towards the house. State Police once reported seeing Mary's wraith crossing the road in front of her house.

In 1917, Louis Roy and his mother purchased the house and opened it to the public for tours at a fee. His claims of Mary's ghost being present in the house captured the attention of everybody from magazines to thrill seekers looking for pirates and treasure. Not only did a rocking chair move back and forth on its own volition when guests walked by it, but Louis, or "Gus" as he was also known, also rented shovels for fifty cents each so people could have a chance at finding the gold Don Pedro had buried in the yard.

Both he and his mother had claimed to see Mary's spirit on many occasions descending the staircase and disappearing into thin air. During the hurricane of 1938, Mr. Roy noticed the garage he had built was swaying dangerously in the wind. He went out and found some long timber to support the sides. When he returned to the safety of his home, his mother asked who was helping him. He was quite shocked as he'd done the job quite alone at the time. She swore she saw a tall red-haired girl in a white gown helping him with the boards. She then started to follow him into the house, but vanished just before crossing the threshold.

Later Mr. Roy would meet the ghost of Mary Wallace again, when a fierce storm overtook the region. He claimed that she saved his life nineteen times during his struggle to hold his buildings together during the great Nor'easter. The Roy family held tours of the house well into the 1960s before it changed hands. David and Corinne Russell then took ownership of the house. Mrs. Russell had cared for Mr. Roy in his old age and knew well of the history of the house, as Mr. Roy told her everything he knew about the now famous landmark. I will divulge those words later. Lets stay with the ghostly encounters for now.

During the Russell's tenure in the house, a caretaker accidentally dropped a kerosene heater down the stairs and caught the wall and staircase on fire. Having no running water in the house, Mr. Russell dashed outside to grab some snow in order to quench the flames. When he returned, the massive fire was out. His wife, watching in disbelief, related how the flames just quickly died down and smothered out. They were sure that the ghost of Mary Wallace had a role in the uncanny occurrence.

People visiting the house have had strange feelings when near the hearthstone of the fireplace. Some claim to have felt vibrations when touching it. One visitor came to the house and was greeted by a tall woman in eighteenth century attire. The woman who answered the door said that the house was a mess and the owners were not home at the time. The guest thought she looked rather strange in appearance, but heeded her words and left. Later, when she returned, she was informed that no such person exists in the house, at least not in the physical realm. The ghostly woman is still reported to this day wandering the grounds of the house. She is often seen by the well in the yard.

That is the legend of Ocean Born Mary. It is perhaps the greatest legend that has ever emanated from the mouths of New Englanders. Behind every legend there is an undeniable quantity of truth that is the basis for its beginning. If the legend has your imagination satisfied, then read no more. If you are curious as to what is truth and what is conjecture, then I urge you to read on and draw your own conclusions in the weaving of fact and fiction that have become the legend of Ocean Born Mary.

It is true that Mary Fulton was born at sea; and yes, she did live in New Hampshire. According to historical records, pirates did raid the *Wolf* off the shores of Boston, but exactly which band of buccaneers remains a mystery to this day. Historians all relate the fact that Mary did wear a wedding gown of green brocaded silk given to her by a pirate. She married James Wallace in 1742, and had four boys and one daughter. Three of the sons settled in Henniker.

The story states that her husband died young. According to record, James Wallace lived to be eighty-one years old. This also might have given birth to the part in the legend where she married Don Pedro who changed his name to James Wallace to escape justice. If Don Pedro was not James Wallace then Mary would have come to live with him while she was seventy-eight years old, which was when her husband actually died. The ex-pirate would be well over one hundred at that point.

It is true that she moved to Henniker, but it was during the final eighteen years of her life. That would be in 1796 when she was seventy-eight years old. She did not live with the pirate Don Pedro at that point. She actually lived with her son, William Wallace. And here is the good part. She never ever lived in the Ocean Born Mary House. That house belonged to her son, Roger Wallace. William's house was about a mile away, but nonetheless, a different home altogether.

I mentioned before about Mr. Roy confiding his experiences in the house to Mrs. Russell. Well, he told her the whole thing was made up based on historical accounts he had read and the spooky atmosphere of the home. There is no treasure in the back yard. There is no pirate buried under the hearth. There is no ghost of Mary Wallace in the (not) Ocean Born Mary House. Yet scores of famous paranormal investigators and psychics have seen and experienced all of the above and more at the historically wrong address. Even the furniture Mr. Roy had claimed belonging to Mary, was bought for the purpose of creating an atmosphere of ghostly illusion for profit. There are even old postcards of the house that have caused it to become the enduring haunted legend that has the curious still scrambling in search of the lost treasure and spirit of one of the most famous stories New England has known.

Some say past and present owners have made up the notion that the house is not the one Mary lived in to stop the thrill seekers from invading their privacy. They are in "cahoots" with the historical society for the purpose of being left alone. Who do you want to believe?

My friend, Mike Carroll, has always been fascinated by the legend—so much so that he even wrote a song about it. Here are a few words:

> "Heave away come and go with me, on the Ocean Born Mary. Heave away come and go with me, all across the rolling seas."

Now I know that the lines suggest that Ocean Born Mary was a ship and not a person, which might in the future add to the dizzying array of accounts already tongued by storytellers. Just remember what you believe in your heart, and the spirit of the tale will always outlive the strict letter of historical fact.

Henniker, New Hampshire is located in the southwestern part of the state. Take Route 89 to Exit 5, Route 9/202. Take Route 114 South into Henniker. The house, cemetery, and Historical Society are along that road, and all information can be gathered at the historical society.

Hillsboro

Bear Hill Road

Sitting ominously on Bear Hill Road is a very old house the locals have dubbed the "Plague House." This is because a long time ago, the residents of the homestead became infected with a plague. Most likely either scarlet fever or consumption (tuberculosis) was the cause, as both were very much feared in the nineteenth century.

The house was sealed and quarantined until the family passed away. The neighbors then carefully removed the remains and buried them far into the woods in deep graves so the animals would not dig them up and spread the infection. Unfortunately, the people who interred the family were not careful enough in their sanitary practices and became contaminated with the disease and died.

The place is now haunted by a white ghost that is reported to actually make itself known when visitors put in an appearance to the foreboding haunted dwelling. Locals have also heard macabre moans and screams coming from the property as the past souls relive the painful agony of their demise. It is reported that no one in the area is brave enough to venture onto the ghoulishly troubled property. The fact that it is also posted as *no trespassing* might be a slight deterrent as well.

If you still want to travel Bear Hill Road there are a few old shacks on the corner of the road that Ghost Quest investigated. It was not their mission at first, but when sensitive Raven became agitated and got an upset stomach while passing the abandoned buildings, it was enough for them to stop and check things out. When they first exited the car, Doug and Raven felt an eerie numbness overcome a portion of their faces. Raven, along with members Doug and Fred, took pictures of the shacks. The place had an ominous ambiance to it that was certainly uninviting. The photographs are posted on their website, www.ghostquest.org for all to see. Perhaps it might be the closest you want to come to Bear Hill Road. Perhaps you are braver…

Bear Hill Road is located in Hillsboro, New Hampshire. Take Interstate Route 93 to Interstate Route 89. Take Exit 5, Route 202/9 into Hillsboro. Bear Hill Road is easy to find from there.

Hollis

Pine Hill Cemetery

As one rambles among the stones of the Pine Hill Cemetery, it becomes quickly evident that this is a very old burial ground. Many of the founding families of Hollis are buried here and a large quantity of stones are either unmarked or have been defaced by the ravages of time and nature. Some have even mysteriously disappeared with the passing of time. No wonder this graveyard is reputed to be extremely haunted.

There are 291 recorded burials in the cemetery dating back to about 1769, when Benjamin Parker sold his farm and decided to deed the rest of his land to the town for a common burying place. It was then that Pine Hill was born for the dead. Do not be fooled by the peaceful little knolls that run amidst the old burial markers, for when the sun begins to set and the twilight sets in, many of Pine Hill's permanent residents take to wandering among their monuments. Scores of paranormal investigators and curious ghost hunters have witnessed the energy and presence of the interred at Pine Hill. Many recordings and photographs have been taken with evidence that the burial ground is not completely at peace.

Of all the ghosts that have been witnessed at Pine Hill, the most common is that of Abel Blood and his family. So much so, that the locals have renamed the necropolis, "Blood Cemetery." Many legends and lore state that the Blood family was murdered, and therefore they are not at rest. As you read on, you will see that the dates on the graves of the Blood family show that they all passed on over a long course of time. All can be assured that the evil deed of murder never took place in the Blood family, save for perhaps as a retelling of the haunted cemetery stories in front of a campfire on a long dark New Hampshire night. Why then, do Abel Blood and his family wander among their tombstones? What are they looking for and why? Perhaps you should read on to find out more.

The Blood family was among the first settlers of Hollis. Elnathan Blood came to Hollis around 1740. He married Elizabeth Boynton in 1741. They were simple folk, farming the lands for their means. On July 13, 1754, they had a son named Abel. A few years later, in 1757, Elnathan served in the French War.

After his tenure as soldier, he came back to the homestead and settled for good. He even served as town selectman in 1773. Early records show that he died around 1789 at about age seventy-two and was buried at

Pine Hill. Unfortunately, the exact whereabouts of his stone is unknown, as his was one of the many markers that succumbed to time and age.

Abel grew up and served in the Continental Army in 1780. He and his wife Sarah had four children. He died on November 1, 1820 at the age of sixty-six years, three months, and nineteen days. Sarah died on February 13, 1852 at age eighty-five. They are both buried in the Blood plot with their children and grandchildren.

One daughter, Betsy, died on May 6, 1861. Her real name is, supposedly, Mehitable, according to town records. Sarah Blood who married Daniel Cram, was born June 9, 1809 and died February 3, 1878 at age seventy-one years, eight months. So far, they seemed to have lived decently long lives for the times. Leonard Blood and his wife were not so fortunate. He died rather young on September 16, 1832. He is listed on the stone of his wife, Hannah, who passed away several years before him on December 23, 1826, at age twenty-seven. There are no children among the three listed.

This brings us to Abel Blood Jr., who is said to be the main haunt of Pine Hill. He was born May 5, 1797, and died January 8, 1867, at age seventy according to his stone. Mentioned on his stone is also his wife,

Pine Hill Cemetery.

Betsy, who died very young on June 1, 1827, at age twenty-six—only two months after giving birth to their only child, George. Tragically George Blood would not survive infancy and died on October 4, 1830, at only three and a half years old.

It could be these heartbreaking events that Abel Blood had persevered in his life that still linger through the centuries. Maybe the souls of those whose graves have disappeared, including Elnathan, are also among those who roam the grounds looking for their eternal claim to immortality. Whatever the case, those who travel to the Blood plot overlooking the cemetery road can feel the restless spirits of the Blood family. Most activity takes place at the Abel Blood stone where investigators have gotten strange noises and even tapping sounds on tape, as if someone was trying to communicate to them in code. His stone is where most people have taken photographs of strange shapes and orbs, as well as other aberrations.

Ghost Quest out of Manchester, New Hampshire, has done several investigations at the spot and has come up with substantial evidence, through EVP recordings (see glossary and equipment explanations) and strange photographs, that the vicinity is indeed haunted. Christine, a sensitive in the group could feel energy around some of the lesser-known graves. Raven became queasy when walking towards the back of the graveyard. This feeling quickly dissipated as she exited from that section.

Our trip to the cemetery was on a beautiful sunny day. The excitement of investigating the famed Pine Hill Cemetery was quite awesome. We followed our usual protocol of touching absolutely nothing, but it seems that others were not so respectful, as the stone of Abel Blood had been broken into several pieces. This was a very upsetting sight, as the highest respect should be given to the deceased and their plots at all times.

Everyone travels that path, and karma has a way of getting back at those disreputable deeds.

We took some pictures and some EVP recordings but nothing came from them. There was an aura of energy that made the compass swing and the EMF (see glossary and equipment explanations) meter buzz a bit. It was probably the spirits still in ire over the ruined stone.

Another eerie phenomenon also occurs at his stone. There is a carving of a hand with the index finger pointing towards the sky. It is said that at night, when one walks by the marker, a most horrifying spectacle is witnessed. The hand is no longer pointing toward heaven, but towards the ground instead. Many who have passed the Blood lot on a moonlit night have attested to this most peculiar vision. What is Abel trying to tell them? Is it that he wants all to know he is still there, or could it be a sign that he is presently out of crypt? If you visit the Pine Hill Cemetery and the finger on Abel Blood's gravestone is no longer aiming towards the sky, keep your senses on high alert. That twig snapping behind you or that tapping noise you thought you heard might just be of Blood relation.

Pine Hill Cemetery is located on Nartoff Road in Hollis, New Hampshire. Take Interstate Route 3 to Exit 6, Route 130. Travel west on Route 130 to Nartoff Road. Bear north onto Nartoff Road and follow to cemetery. Pine Hill is open from dawn to dusk, so please obey all rules and regulations posted, as it is also patrolled regularly.

Blood family plot. Note Abel's vandalized stone in the background.

Isles of Shoals

As the frequent dips of my pen into the inkwell fortify this narration, I can attest to not being as much of a connoisseur of pirate folklore as I have now become. Being a native New Englander, my love of the sea and its accouterments is natural. After visiting the Isles of Shoals, that esteem for the deep and those who are responsible for making the fearful shudder in the restless coastal storms, has grown considerably.

As Arlene and I boarded the *M/V Thomas Laighton* for the rocky outcroppings that sit ten miles off the coast of Portsmouth, we had no idea what to expect. It is always better to be at least a little astonished at what lies ahead in this aspect of ghost hunting. There are nine islands: Duck Island, Appledore, Malaga, Smuttynose, and Cedar Island are property of Maine. Star Island, Lunging, Seavey's, and White hail from New Hampshire. These are the four islands that hold our interest at the moment.

The history of the islands is voluminous but I will give you a small timeline to satisfy your appetite for now. In the late 1500s, European fishermen came to the rocky outcroppings and named them after the abundance of fish in the area. In 1605, Champlain is the first to mention the isles in his journals. In 1614, Captain John Smith sails upon the islands and is overwhelmed by their allure. He names them "Smythe's Islands." In 1647, the first official township is created on Hog Island. It is called Appledore, after a town in Devonshire, England. From the late 1600s to the early 1700s, the islands became the home and safe haven for many famous pirates, including Captain Kidd, Captain Quelch, Ned Lowe, Blackbeard, and even Phillip Babb, who lived on the islands and became constable there. His family is buried on Appledore, as that became his permanent home. He died there in 1671, and is said to haunt the cove named after him. He is seen in a butcher's frock wielding a large knife. Countless witnesses have been frightened by their encounter with the angry ghost of Phillip Babb.

In 1715, Gosport, a fishing village is established on Star Island. In 1820, the first lighthouse is erected on White Island. In 1839, Thomas Laighton becomes light keeper of the White Island light. His daughter, Celia Laighton-Thaxter would go on to write the most comprehensive books on the Isles of Shoals, from every aspect possible. In 1848, Mr. Laighton establishes the Appledore House and renames the island at that point. The first ferry service to the isles is also launched the same year.

In 1861, the islands were closed to outsiders due to fear of Confederate invasion. This lasted right up to the end of the Civil War in 1865. In the same year, the present lighthouse was built on White Island. In 1873, two Norwegian women are murdered on Smuttynose. It was reported that a German fisherman, Louis Wagner, killed Karen and Anethe Christenson

Oceanic Hotel where guests report sightings of ghostly pirates and women.

with an axe. Wagner was a lodger at the house of John and Maren Hontvet where the women were killed. He proclaimed his innocence all the way to the gallows, where he hung for the deed on June 18, 1875. That same year, the Oceanic Hotel on Star Island opened to greet visitors to the isles and has provided that same service ever since.

Although the New Hampshire coast can still be seen from the islands, one cannot help but feel completely isolated upon setting anchor in the shoals. Don't worry; you are never completely alone on the rocky land masses, for spirits of the sea still roam eternally in wait or want along the shores and rocky bluffs. Lunging Island is the site of the ghost of one of Blackbeard's wives. This claim comes from the only family residing on the island. Prudy Crandall-Randall's family bought the island in the 1920s. She had grown up hearing the stories of the buried treasure, and how Edward Teach, better known as Blackbeard, left it where the high tide separates the island in half. He also left his thirteenth wife (some say fifteenth), Martha Herring, after his honeymoon with her in 1720 on nearby Smuttynose, to guard the treasure of Lunging while he sailed off to South Carolina. There he met his friend's daughter and fell in love with her, bringing disaster and death in his wake of affection. He was double-crossed by this same friend, who was, at the time, a governor of South Carolina. It was this partner in crime who left him with twenty slashes and gunshot wounds during a struggle at sea. He was then decapitated and his head hung from the prow of a Royal Navy ship for all to see. This was after the governor had pardoned the hardened pirate for his evil deeds.

His wife on Lunging was left to the elements. She died in 1735, after waiting fifteen years for him to return, and is seen to this day wandering along the rocky shore reciting the words, "HE WILL COME BACK." There are also stories of the same ghostly apparition on Appledore, as well as Star and White Islands. Records indicate that Martha bounced from island to island while living there, so it is entirely possible that she still roams the various landmasses the same as she did in life.

Star Island is home to Betty Moody's Cave. The story is told that Betty Moody, a resident of the island, found refuge in a cave during an Indian raid. She and her two children hid in fear of their lives. While holed up in the cavern, the children began to whimper. She covered their mouths so hard that she suffocated them. Some say she did it to spare her own life. Whatever version you deem valid does not take away from the fact that she is eternally sorrowful for her actions, as screams and wails can be heard from the cave where she mourns her fateful act. Shortly following the creepy bellows, comes a terrible storm. When one hears the unearthly wails of the Isles of Shoals Banshee, it is wise to take cover and stay moored, for it is assured that foolish mariners who heed not the moans of ill omen will be sent to the bottom of the sea.

Lunging Island's only house, where residents say Blackbeard's treasure is still watched over by his phantom wife.

White Island is reported to host two quarreling ghosts. They are heard arguing in the wind, yet there are no physical forms to be seen creating the voices that banter back and forth. Footsteps are also heard around the island, as the residents of the past still ramble along the rocks and walkways. Another famous ghost of the Shoals is that of a fisherman who took revenge years after his demise to the sea. Legend has it that "guinea boats" manned by Portuguese and Italian sailors were known to frequent the islands. One day, a crewmember of such a boat saw a fisherman's wife in her yard. In a drunken stupor, he accosted her. As she fought off his advances, the sailor threw the woman to the ground and plunged a knife into her chest. When he boarded his boat, his mates were aware of the man's dastardly deed, but lay quiet as the boat sailed for Boston.

The husband was accused of the crime, as the couple frequently fought with each other. When police arrived from the mainland, a great storm blew up and stranded them on the island for the night. Sometime around midnight, the prisoner jumped out of the window of his home and scurried towards a dory. There, in the rage of the storm, did he make his getaway at sea. The man and boat were never seen again, or so they say.

Some months later, the same crew returned to the island as routine would have it. That night a fog rolled in and the boat, anchored in the harbor, became enveloped in the eerie mist. Suddenly, the air was saturated with the most horrifying screams radiating from the sleeping quarters of the ship. When the rest of the crew rushed below, they found the crewmember that had murdered the woman waving the bloody stump of his arm. Someone, or something, had chopped off his hand at the wrist. Other members on deck heard the dunking of oars in the water and saw a vaporous figure in a dory rowing away from the vessel.

After that hideous night, no guinea boat was ever safe in the isles. Each time there, a crewmember would suffer some sort of mutilation. One had an ear lopped off. Another had a foot chopped off, and still another sailor had an eye torn from his socket. Each time, the ghastly deed was followed by the solemn sound of oars swishing the water as the ghost dory slowly rowed off into the fog. If one is squeamish over such events, then check your heritage before visiting the isles. The fisherman was never found, but it seems he was never lost.

White Island where the spirits of two men whine in the wind at each other.

The ghost ship, *Isidore,* is seen on occasion sweeping by the Isle of Shoals from Rye to Portsmouth. Those who encounter the ship while at sea, rush for safe haven. Those who witness it from land, hastily batten down the hatches, for surely a storm of evil corollary is just over the horizon. As these accounts unfold in front of you, it must come to light that ghosts of the cursed isles come in many forms. This is what makes the Isles of Shoals a magical place to visit—apparently, from both sides of the veil.

The Isles of Shoals can be accessed by the Isles of Shoals Steamship Company at 315 Market Street, Portsmouth, New Hampshire 03801. 800-441-4620 or 603-431-5500.

Take Interstate Route 95 to Exit 7, Market Street, Portsmouth. Bear right at bottom of exit and follow right to steamship dock.

A view of the haunted islands from a few miles away.

Keene

The Eternal Vigil of Harriet Huntress:
Keene State College

Harriet Lane Huntress is ageless. This is due to the fact that her academic achievements have been honored by naming a hall at Keene State College after her.

Huntress Hall was erected in 1926. Harriet was actually responsible for the building of the hall. It was originally built as a dorm for the women of the college. With the advent of World War II, it became necessary to convert it into a housing for men who were training for battle. It now houses 150 residents who swear night and day that there is one more permanent dweller that can be heard in the otherwise quiet of the night. That other tenant is Harriet Lane Huntress herself.

Harriet Huntress was an invaluable supporter of the college during her lengthy tenure as part of the State Office of Education. It would seem fitting to honor her with such a dignitary testament to her support of Keene and its students. During her later years, it was reported that she proudly roamed the halls of her namesake in her wheelchair, as she surely loved her building. Even now, she seems to still roam the same halls many years after she has physically left the realm of the living.

Residents have reported the scraping sounds of a wheelchair coming from the upper floor of the hall. In the dark bowers of the night, the creaking of a chair can be heard slowly succeeding down the hallways as Harriet Huntress makes her endless rounds, still admiring the building that bears her name. A strange fact about the hall is that her actual wheelchair still resides in the attic. It has to, for how else would she get around in these times? Harriet Huntress is not the only resident ghost of the hall. It seems there might be another spirit, perhaps from the time of World War II, still hanging about the building.

Resident and Keene student, Amy Patryn, told me that a friend of hers, Kara, who lives in the hall a few rooms away, was reading one night while her roommate slept. She looked over and saw a misty figure of a man sitting on the end of the bed. The apparition was glowing. She closed her eyes a few times and even looked away to make sure she was not imagining things. The manifestation still lingered on the bed. All at once, it vanished into the darkness. On another occasion, she entered her room and saw the same apparition crouched by the same bed. It then vanished, same as before.

Huntress Hall has three living floors, an attic, and a basement. It is also the site of a haunted tour around Halloween. It is known as one of the most haunted campuses in the United States. Harriet Huntress makes herself quite known to this day. If you are in Huntress Hall and hear the creaking and scraping of a wheelchair echoing through the corridors, show some consideration and move aside. It may be your area for a short time, but it is hers forever.

Keene State College is located at 229 Main Street, Keene, New Hampshire 03435.

Take Route 101 West into Keene. At second light, bear right onto Main Street. Bear left onto Wyman Way then take a left into visitor's parking lot. A walkway across from the parking lot leads to the Fiske Quadrangle. Take a left at the quadrangle, and Huntress Hall is directly ahead at end of quadrangle. The college was also once the site of an old hospital, so take that into consideration as well.

Laconia

Colonial Theatre

Main Street in Downtown Laconia is bustling with interesting shops and restaurants that spring to life with the rising of the sun, and dwindle with the pale of the moon. Sitting among these little gems for tourists, is a lone building void of life during the day. Come nightfall, when the moon's faint glow beams down upon its doors, something unworldly churns inside this now defunct theatre. Spirits spring to life, reliving the days of silent movies and Vaudeville acts. Doors open and close as they did when the place was peopled, and lights turn on and off. Footsteps can be heard echoing down the empty aisles and hallways, and even the sinister shade of a man can be seen in the shadows of the unlit playhouse. How would one know this from a theatre that is now closed? The answer is simple. These events went on even when the building was bustling with patrons filling the seats every night for a show or movie.

When the theatre opened in 1915, it was hailed as a far more extravagant playhouse than the small town of Laconia could ever need. The Laconia Democrat referred to it as one of the most beautiful theaters in all New England. It boasted the likes of silent movies, Vaudeville shows, and even the music of John Phillip Sousa. As time went on, its diversity diminished until only movies were seen there. Then came the fateful day, after eighty-six years of entertaining the masses, that it closed its doors for good.

Now, when the dusk beckons the later hours, all revelry is left to the spirits that have stayed behind to see one more eternal show that time has long canned and shelved. Perhaps, if you are in the area of the Colonial Theatre, you might peer into the dusty windows and see the ghosts opening and closing the doors on their way to the ethereal seats that await them. Or you might catch a sound of the act in progress, as it trails off into the void of the afterworld.

The Colonial Theatre is located at 611 Main Street, Laconia, New Hampshire 03246. Take Interstate Route 93 to Exit 20, Route 3 North to Laconia. Once in Laconia, Route 3 becomes Main Street.

Old Streetcar Place

Laconia is a great place for the passing tourist to stop, shop, and absorb some history. In fact, the oldest unaltered brick knitting mill, the Belknap Mill—built in 1823—is located in Laconia. Of course, there are other historic buildings to enjoy. Some have been altered to fit the times, and some still have the ghosts of their times to keep their history "alive," so to speak.

Take the Old Streetcar Place which once housed a factory that produced—you guessed it—streetcars. These now archaic modes of transportation were the forerunners of bus lines and subways. The factory in Laconia built and shipped these cars all over the United States. With the passing of the streetcar, so came the decline of the building. It now houses some state offices on the second floor and various other businesses, not to forget a few residual inhabitants from other lifetimes, as well.

Employees staying late have heard coughs, footsteps, and even voices coming from numerous areas throughout the building. As the pensive individual searched for another living being, it became evident that they were quite alone in the building—or were they? If there were several members of staff in the structure, they might all look at each other in unpleasant wonder over who was causing the phantom clamor.

Though no one knows who the otherworldly culprits are, they all have stated one common fact. The noises start up around the same time that the second shift historically came on in the old factory when it produced the streetcars. Phones are known to ring, and when answered, produce an eerie static from the other end. Doors open and close by themselves, as well. These events have actually compelled even the most skeptical of workers to shy from late night duties while alone in the building.

Some jobs are a lifelong quest. I guess the occupation of building streetcars goes way beyond that which we can understand. In this life, anyway.

Old Streetcar Place is located at 63 Beacon Street in Laconia, New Hampshire 03246. Follow above directions to Beacon Street and the building is easy to spot.

Crazy Gringo Restaurant

The original building in question served as a grocery store owned by George Weeks. Later proprietors included George W. Tarlson, W.T. Cram, and Oscar Hall under the ownership of Arthur C. Kinsman. Mr. Tarlson purchased the store in 1895. Early in the twentieth century, he moved his business across the street. The old building burned and was later torn down. The present structure was rebuilt for the sole purpose of becoming a diner and boarding house. Although the original edifice is gone, it seems some of the entities have stayed behind.

A woman's voice is heard in the dining room and kitchen. Doors are known to unlock by themselves and swing open while witnesses stand agape. Apparitions have been seen wandering around a hallway on the second floor near the back porch. It seems, perhaps, the families that ran the store and lived upstairs still have some unfinished business in that spot, or are just as happy with the new building as they were with the old one. We were given a tour of the building, and though we felt a little excited, nothing out of the ordinary happened at that time.

Present owner Mike Daly told me in an interview that *he* has not seen anything out of the ordinary yet, but his employees have a lot to tell. Some of them lived in the rooms above the restaurant during the busy summer months. At various times of the day and night, they were witness to the wandering apparition upstairs. They named one of the ghosts "Uncle Charlie" after the person who rebuilt the edifice in 1925. Mike had T-shirts made for the restaurant depicting the building with the ghost of Uncle Charlie looking out a third floor window, as if watching over his place.

There were also a few suicides in the building during its tenure as a boarding house. This might have a lot to do with the ghosts of the Crazy Gringo. There have been sightings of a ghost in the second floor right corner window where one of the tragic demises took place. The ghosts of the building are active at times, but the upstairs is vacant for the most part during the off-season winter months. If ghosts are wandering in the witching hours during the cold months, they go unnoticed. All that said, it is assured that the cuisine is out of this world and so are some of the residents.

The Crazy Gringo Restaurant, where the ghosts of Uncle Charlie and others from the past still roam its walls.

The Crazy Gringo is located at 306 Lakeside Avenue at Weirs Beach in Laconia, New Hampshire 03247. Follow directions to the Winnipesaukee Marketplace noted in the following section.

Bedroom window where ghost of a former tenant is seen.

Inside the haunted bedroom at the Crazy Gringo.

The Winnipesaukee Marketplace

George Weeks had an idea. There was a lake and people. Bring them together with lodging, and the outcome is a summer resort. In 1887, he built a small eight-room addition to a Methodist boarding house. In 1880, he erected a hotel, and by 1899, the Lakeside House was a full-blown seventy-five-room resort with a spacious dining hall.

Mr. Weeks welcomed guests by train to the hotel overlooking Lake Winnipesaukee for many years. From June to October, accommodations were second to none. There was also a billiards hall, a small casino, and, as expected, lots of water activities. George Weeks was in charge of it all. It appears, though, that he has never fully relinquished his position. The hotel became a marketplace in the 1990s, according to the Lake Winnipesaukee Historical Society. Even long after the demise of the Lake House, George Weeks still makes his rounds.

Cold spots have been experienced by guests and employees alike. Although the hotel is gone, the patrons of the marketplace still encounter incidents of spirits trying to manifest themselves in a more physical form. On certain nights, it is said that the shade of a man who hung himself in the hotel can be seen in a third floor window. The specters of a man and woman are occasionally spied wandering through sections of the building. Perhaps it is George Weeks and his wife still wandering through their hotel in an attempt to greet guests. Or, perhaps they are confused as to what has become of their grand resort.

Either way, the ghosts are there, and in the tradition of the hotel-turned-marketplace, waiting to greet you as well.

The Winnipesaukee Marketplace is located at 1 Weeks Street at Weirs Beach, New Hampshire 03247. Take Interstate Route 93 to Exit 23, Route 104 in Meredith. Follow Route 104 to the end. Take right to Weirs Beach. The famous marketplace is easy to spot.

Winnipesaukee Marketplace, where some guests have never fully checked out. Old railroad tracks still run along the side of the former hotel.

Weirs Beach General Store

While taking some of the photographs of Weirs Beach, it became necessary to purchase more film. The general store sits right in the middle of the street. As a matter of fact, it is the same store that George W. Tarlson moved across the street in 1915. The original building was a small barn or storage shed. It was transformed into a store, and has been ever since.

Present owner Mike Houle is a friendly, straight-forward person. We mentioned our purpose in the area and he began to tell us of another haunted site at Weirs Beach—his store. The store is haunted by the spirit of Crazy Moe. Who was Crazy Moe? It was a cat. It did not start out as his pet and friend. At first it was a ferrule feline that he fed. As time went on, the cat began to slowly wander into the establishment through the back room. Before long, Crazy Moe was purring on the counter to patrons of the general store.

Crazy Moe lived with Mike for seven years before he passed away. Mike knew that the cat loved the building, so he wanted to bury him near the stairs outside. He put the cat in a freezer while he made preparations for a proper burial. After the interment, it became evident that Moe was not ready to be forgotten. The familiar sound of Moe's mews began to saturate the back room of the store. This is where Moe would sleep and eat. Many searches for a feline would prove fruitless, as the room would be vacant of any living creature.

It appears that Moe is still making his presence known to the store. Even the freezer, which was in perfect working order, will not shut tightly. The door opens upwards and Mike has had to put heavy items on it to keep it from popping up. It is more a prop now than anything else.

Many people believe that animals cannot come back as ghosts. There are too many instances, much like the Weirs Beach General Store's phantom mouser, to wag your tail at.

The store is located next to the Winnipesaukee Marketplace. Follow directions mentioned prior to Weirs Beach.

Weirs Beach General Store is the eternal home for the spirit of Crazy Moe.

Litchfield

Cemetery With No Bodies

As strange as the title may sound, it is true. As you read the next narrative, it will become logically clear why this eerie burial ground has no buried. The western frame of Litchfield is located along the banks of the Merrimack River. The scenic sensations of this flowing tributary are boundless to the eye. There is a section along Route 3A where the great river bottlenecks. This is the site of a former Presbyterian Church.

Along with the church, sat the village burial ground, laid out along the banks of the river. In the early 1800s, there was a terrible flood that washed away the caskets and bodies of the cemetery. The townspeople recovered some of the heavier stones. In 1843, the town officials moved those stones across the street behind the new church. The lost markers were recreated from memory and existing family monuments. That is why many of the markers look exactly alike, despite the difference in years. The fact that many of them are so close together is also a testament of proof that no one is interred next to the stones. Although the dead do not rest there, it is reported that they do seem to reside in the graveyard, for there is a great amount of energy floating around the stones.

New England Ghost Project has done a few investigations there. EVP specialist Karen Mossey captured a voice that was not happy of their presence in the churchyard.

When she asked them if they were present, something answered "Just Leave…Get Out!" They also got some orbs floating around, but the recording really gave them some evidence that the dead have returned to claim their ground.

When we visited the cemetery, it was an overcast day. Rain was in the forecast and the cold air sent chills of a most arctic nature through the late morning air. The stillness among the graves was unnerving. It was as if the spirits were dormant but cautiously watching us as we took pictures and EVP recordings. There were no ghost voices to be heard that day. They may have been tired, perhaps after a busy night of revelry.

If you decide to trek into Litchfield and visit the empty graveyard, please give it the same utmost respect you would any other cemetery. Just because there are no bodies does not mean that no*body* is there.

The cemetery is located on Route 3A in Litchfield, New Hampshire. Take Everett Turnpike to Exit 2, Sagamore Bridge Road. Follow over the

Merrimack River, then bear left onto Route 3A. Follow into Litchfield. White church is just past Griffin Memorial School on right next to a fire station. The cemetery is behind the church.

Cemetery with no bodies in Litchfield.

Griffin Memorial School

This area seems to house a lot of residual energy. As we pulled up to the school, we felt a bit more tingly than usual. Maybe it was the fact that we were at another haunted place. Maybe it was more. Arlene and I took a few shots of the outside of the school, and I narrated what I had heard from historians and paranormal groups. The haunting of the school is due to a few efficient ghosts, or one boisterous poltergeist. Maintenance crews have experienced some strange phenomena over the years. While cleaning up at night, they have heard desks in other rooms scraping across the floor. When they investigate, they find them arranged in strange patterns. Voices and noises have hastened the after hours duties by some of the team, as they know they are alone in the building when these occurrences begin.

Although these might be enough to raise the hairs of the bravest, it was the ball field that was of particular interest. It is said that a young child accidentally hung himself while climbing the fence of the playing field behind the school. His specter is now seen roaming the area where he suffered his most unfortunate fate. Many witnesses have claimed to have seen the phantom child on warm nights when the stars cast a dim light on the ground, and the shadows show the child figure eternally playing among the rings of steel that surround the haunted field.

Griffin Memorial School.

As we wandered around the field taking readings and snapping pictures, I looked up through the trees and saw in the distance, the white steeple of a meeting house. That was where the cemetery with no bodies was located but a half mile away. One cannot help but wonder if that had anything to do with the goings on at the school, and if the woods between them have something to say as well.

Griffin Memorial School is located on Route 3A in Litchfield, New Hampshire. Follow directions mentioned prior for Cemetery With No Bodies. The school is about one half mile before the cemetery on right.

Haunted field behind school.

Roy Memorial Park—Darrah Pond

As the suns rolls below the trees of Roy Memorial Park, the murky waters of Darrah Pond begin to echo with the cries of a child screaming for help. This is not a scene out of a horror movie, but one that is played out many nights to the residents and visitors of the park where the haunted pond sits charmingly, yet foreboding, within its perimeter. No one knows who the desperate ghost is, but his phantom utterances send chills through those whose ears fall within range of the occurrence.

Roy Memorial Park is a quaint little spread of land with two playgrounds and, of course, the pond. During our visit to the park, we encountered several families playing with their young on the swings and slides. They were aware of the watery specter, but have never actually seen the ghost. They also knew when the twilight hours enveloped the land, the playgrounds became uninhabited of living beings. It seems no one wants to see the ghost of the child in the pond. We took some photographs and voice recordings, but it was in the early afternoon. The ghostly activity occurred at night. We could not wait around that long. Or, maybe we wisely chose *not* to.

Darrah Pond is located in Roy Memorial Park, Litchfield, New Hampshire. Follow directions mentioned earlier but bear right onto Pinecrest Road before Griffin Memorial School. Follow Pinecrest Road to Albuquerque Avenue. Bear right onto Albuquerque Avenue and then left into Roy Memorial Park. Darrah Pond is directly ahead.

Foreboding view of Darrah Pond, where phantom cries still permeate the night air.

Littleton

Beal House Inn and Restaurant

This next account is presented exactly as I received it. The letter documents the haunting of the Beal House Inn and Restaurant as experienced by owners Catherine and Jose Luis Pawelek. It is so interesting, that I am confident the reader will enjoy its contents exactly as it was presented to me. Here it is.

"Dear Mr. D'Agostino:

Thank you for your enquiry. When we purchased the Beal House Inn and Restaurant in 2001, one of the first e-mails we received was from a former innkeeper, who asked whether we had encountered the ghost yet.

What a surprise. We did not read much into it, except for the following event. Three months after our move to the Inn, my parents came to visit from Europe, and at breakfast the first morning, my mother said, "Now that you own an inn, you have to be more considerate of your guests and be quiet when you go up and down the stairs in the middle of the night and not slam the doors." When she told me that she had heard all this at around 1:30 in the morning, I was able to tell her that it was not us, as we were fast asleep on the other side of the house, and with no other guests in the house that night, it could only have been the ghost, that the former owner had talked about.

The following year, while in the middle of renovations, our housekeeper was busy painting one of the guest room's window trim. All of a sudden, she felt a hand on her hip with pressure in one direction (as if somebody was pushing her aside to pass by). Thinking it was one of us (as we had been coming and going into the room all day), she turned around to move aside, but was not able to move her hip for a couple of seconds. Neither of us were standing behind her. She finally caught her breath and resumed painting. When a few minutes had passed, the same occurrence took place on her other side. After regaining her composure, she ran to find us in order to immediately tell us what had occurred.

During the coming year, we had additional minor events happen but the following more intricate event took place in 2003, when we had two couples staying with us at the inn. While the women went into town to shop, the men stayed behind in the common room to have afternoon tea in front of the wood-burning fire. As good friends, they were just relaxing and felt they did not have to say much, but were enjoying the peace and quiet. All of a sudden, they both heard a male voice, saying something unintelligible, they simultaneously looked up and asked one another, "What did you say?" It was clear that neither had spoken, and when a few minutes later they heard the voice again, they intercommed us to tell us their encounter with the ghost.

Subsequently, we had a single woman stay at the inn, and the next morning at breakfast, she told as that in the middle of the night she had felt a presence at the end of the bed in her room, and when she opened her eyes, there was a woman standing at the end of the bed whispering to her and beckoning her. Initially, she thought it was I, but then everything dissipated. After she told us her story, she relayed the fact that she was a medium and had a strong feeling when she entered the inn the day before to check in. She added that it was a strong positive aura and benevolent "good" feelings.

A couple of months ago while I was doing some paperwork in the dining room, I heard a mumble and saw a fleeting shadow in the lower level of the restaurant. Thinking it was my husband, returning from the grocery store, I called out to him, but received no answer. I looked outside and did not notice his car, so I checked downstairs but there was nobody there. I resumed my paperwork when a warm rush passed over me from behind, as if somebody had passed by me, but there was nobody there.

We feel that there is a good presence protecting and watching over us.

Regards,

Catherine and Jose Luis Pawelek,
Chefs/Innkeepers, Beal House Inn and Restaurant, Littleton, NH 03561."

Who exactly are the ghosts of the Beal House Inn? Maybe it is the spirit of Mrs. Beal who turned the place into an inn in 1933. One of the rooms is named after her. Maybe it is any one of the residents who lived in the house since it was built as a farmhouse in 1833. Maybe it is Mr. McGrady, Mrs. Beal's second husband who lodged there one night in 1940, before becoming wooed by the lady owner. Maybe it is all of them. With an inn of such charm and peaceful tranquility, I can understand why no one would ever want to leave.

The Beal House Inn and Restaurant is located at 2 West Main Street, Littleton, New Hampshire 03561. 603-444-2661. Take Interstate Route 93 to Exit 41. Take a right at the end of ramp. Travel one-half mile into Littleton to the junction of Route 302 and Route 18. The inn is on your right. Excellent accommodations, great food, and "spirits" make this place a must on your list.

Manchester

Bob Shaw's Italian Sandwich Shop

Linda Shaw, owner of Bob Shaw's, is not afraid of her ghost. As a matter of fact, the two other co-workers think it is rather entertaining to have an otherworldly presence around. They do not think of it as a ghost as much as a poltergeist. Either way, it seems to have made permanent residence in the building.

Bob Shaw's Italian Sandwich Shop.

The sub shop was formerly called Psaris Bistro. Previous owners complained of names being called out from thin air and noises that were unexplainable, such as pans falling or someone bumping into items that would move or fall. They also saw shadows move across the mirrors in the dining area. The previous owners called the entity "Avery." It is unclear why that particular name was given to the spirit. These strange occurrences might seem a bit unsettling for a quiet sub shop.

I spoke with Linda, and she told me that activity is spontaneous. They never know when their invisible friend is going to make a scene. Recently, all three of the staff on duty witnessed the meat thermometer fly out of the cup it was kept in and land three feet away on a table. Items fly off the shelves at random when no visible entity is there to catapult them. They have even put utensils down for but a moment, only to turn back and notice they have disappeared. The next day, they might come in and find the items right where they had placed them last. One day, an employee was slicing meat in the kitchen. As he cut the slices, he stacked them neatly. At one point, he looked over at his work and was astonished to see that that the piles of deli fare were thrown about the kitchen. No one visible could have entered the room and grabbed the freshly cut meat without him seeing them.

Linda played several EVP recordings that were taken in the restaurant at different locations. One was taken in the kitchen, another in the back of the sandwich shop, and one more upstairs where she lived. The voices and exact syllables on some were hard to distinguish. The others were clear and concise. One says, "IT'S MIKE." Another rings, "IT'S HIM." One more states, "WHO SHOT HIM?" or "MICHELLE." She keeps them on hand for customers to hear if they are brave enough to listen.

The apartment upstairs is also the focus of ghostly activity. There was one incident where a showerhead that had been turned on mysteriously, turned itself up towards the ceiling spraying water all over the bathroom. The occurrence left the bathroom a mess and the poor woman a bit unnerved. Although you cannot visit the apartments, you can still get a chance to witness flying *whatnot* for yourself, as you take in a sample of the delicious fare. The menu says that it is the home of "real" Maine Italian soups, sandwiches, and comfort food. No one knows who the spirit is or why it is haunting the place. Could it be that it likes Italian?

Bob Shaw's Italian Sandwich Shop is located at 915 Elm Street, Manchester, New Hampshire 03101. 603-622-3723. Take Everett Turnpike to Exit 4, Route 3A. Follow Route 3A East a short distance to Route 3/Elm Street. Bear left onto Elm Street. The shop is open Monday through Friday from 8 a.m. to 4 p.m.

Owners and guests have reported shadows moving in these dining room mirrors at Bob Shaw's Restaurant.

Hesser College

It seems that every college has its haunts, or if you will, spirit. Many of these institutions are housed in historic buildings that have etched countless events into their walls. Some are very tragic. At Hesser College, the ghosts roaming the halls of the once old factory are a bit smaller than one would usually encounter. They are children.

Why would ghosts of children be roaming an old factory? The answer lies in history. Many factories employed child labor, as it was cheap, and the children could sustain longer hours than the elderly. It is also because many families needed every able body to bring in any kind of wages. Especially during the Great Depression.

The college was actually founded in 1900, by Joel Hesser. The institution moved several times during the twentieth century, until it finally came to rest at Sundial Avenue. The spirits however, are not at rest. Students and faculty alike hear the bouncing of balls in the corridors of the college as well as footsteps and the revelry of children playing.

As the story goes, the building was once a mill in the early twentieth century. There was a fire in the sub-basement where the child laborers were toiling. The children died in the blaze, and it is those young souls that now rove through the building looking for attention and merriment from their plight in life. The sound of balls bouncing in the back stairwell and footsteps when no doors have been opened or closed can be rather unnerving. The voices and sounds of the ethereal children playing on the fourth floor are frightening. The fact that female students will not take showers alone after midnight due to the strange howling sounds that emanate from the bathroom is downright chilling.

One of the most disturbing stories is that of a woman who supposedly died of hypothermia outside the building and attempted to write help on one of the windows. Students have claimed to hear her frozen fingers squeaking on the windows and a pair of glowing blue eyes peering in from the other side of the glass. There is also the sound of a woman's high heel shoes heard tapping on one of the upper floors on occasion. Even though the floor is carpeted. Is it all legend or initiation stories? Let the children be your guide—even if you can't see them.

Hesser College is located on Sundial Avenue, Manchester, New Hampshire 03101 along the Merrimack River. Take Everett Turnpike to Exit 4. Take a right onto Second Street. Take a right onto Route 3A and travel over Queen City Bridge. Hesser College and Sundial Avenue will be on right.

Hesser College, where the ghosts of children and other entities still linger.

R. G. Sullivan Building

Manchester was once home to the leading cigar manufacturer in New England. R. G. Sullivan had a beautiful Queen Anne-style home that he built in 1892 in the city. He also had a building at 724 Elm Street where the leisure vice of the day was created. Around 1900, he realized that his factory was too small for the demand of his cigars, and built a new structure, in 1913, at 175 Canal Street. The building was called the 7-20-4 Company in honor of the first address his business hailed from. That name still graces the brick edifice to this very day.

Apparently, child labor was used in the manufacturing of these cigars. Those who work in the building still hear the cries of the young reverberating throughout the five available floors now used for office space. Turn of the century factory work was harsh and tedious. Child labor was common and not rewarding. Many tragic incidents left the children maimed or worse in these often unsafe labor conditions.

Time still rings with the proof of these conditions in the R. G. Sullivan Building. Doors also inexplicably open and slam shut throughout the offices. Perhaps the children are trying to tell the present people of the building something. The years have come and gone, and working environments have certainly changed with age. Hopefully the children realize that, and can soon cry no more.

The R.G. Sullivan 7-20-4 Company sits at 175 Canal Street, Manchester, New Hampshire 03101. Take Everett Turnpike to Exit 6, Amoskeag Street. Bear right onto Canal Street. The building is at the corner of Canal Street and West Central Street.

River Road

The place, River Road. The time, about 2:00 a.m. It is serene in the dark hours of early morning and the pavement is void of travelers. Suddenly, that tranquility is broken by the sound of footsteps clopping along the road. Out of nowhere appears a jogger in red shorts and sweatshirt. The white-haired man is completely oblivious to the surrounding hum of the throng that is now gathering to witness this spectacle. It is not a marathon as one might think, but the eternal run of one man unknown to the countless witnesses who have congregated each night to experience, often for the first time, the ghost jogger of River Road.

Curious onlookers have witnessed, and even tried to interact, with the running specter whose expression and gaze remains unchanged as he rambles down the street into the dark void. The next tolling of the two o'clock bell brings the spirit to life again in his eerie nightly vigil. He is witnessed running in the rain, freezing cold, and snow. In an account to the latter, it has been noted that the phantom runs his course leaving not a single print in the snow to follow.

Who is this nocturnal runner and why does he persist on his nightly ritual? Perhaps it is a remnant of a moment in the person's life when he felt most at peace with his world—a world he has refused to leave behind. If you can catch up to him some dark night, ask him. But try not to follow him too far, for where he vanishes to, no one knows, and it can be sure that no one wants to run that trail.

River Road is located near the Merrimack River in Manchester, New Hampshire. Take Interstate Route 93 to Exit 9, Hooksett Road South. Bear right onto Webster Street then another right onto River Road. River Road is about three miles long so pick a spot and good luck.

Merrimack

Matthew Thornton House/
Hannah Jack Tavern/Common Man Restaurant

This seems to be the house with many names and many ghosts as well. The name Hannah Jack comes from the wife of Matthew Thornton, one of the three New Hampshire men who signed the Declaration of Independence. Thornton was born in Ireland in 1714, and migrated to New England as a child. He lived a good portion of his life in Derry, where he served as a doctor. He also served in the New Hampshire Troops in 1745, was a Colonel in the Londonderry Militia until 1775, Associate Justice of the New Hampshire Supreme Court, and Speaker of the House of Representatives for New Hampshire. When the Revolutionary War broke out, he was much to old to actively serve—although he did retain his rank as Colonel.

In 1779, he left his medical practice and retired. In 1780, he moved to Merrimack, where he purchased an estate that was seized by the Continental Congress from Edward Goldstone Lutwyche. It seems Lutwyche was a Tory. A Tory was a British sympathizer during the war. He must have really made some waves for the estate to be taken from his possession.

During all of this activity, Thornton managed to marry Hannah Jack in 1740. They had five children—James, Andrew, Hannah, Matthew, and Mary. Hannah died on December 5, 1786, at the age of forty-four. Their son Andrew died one year later in 1787, at the age of twenty-one. Mathew Thornton died in Newburyport, Massachusetts on June 24, 1803, at the age of eighty-nine while visiting his daughter. He and his family are buried across the street from the house in the Matthew Thornton Cemetery. Both the cemetery and house were placed in the National Register of Historical Places in 1978.

In the early 1800s, his son James turned the home into a tavern. Since then, it has been a private residence, apartments, doctor's office, a restaurant, and, of course, a haunted house.

One of the reported ghosts is that of a man in old clothes seen on occasion. He appears and disappears at random. His identity is unknown. Employees of the restaurant have reported figures meandering past doorways and strange noises in places where there are no living entities to cause them. They also have witnessed shadow people wander by while in the dining area. Shadow people are those figures that are seen out of the corner of a person's eye. There are a lot of explanations for shadow people phenomena. Some say that the rods and cones of the eye can pick up spirit forms that cannot normally be seen by looking directly at the apparition. Others claim it is a bending of light that creates the figures as they move through the corner of one's eye. There are lots of studies to read about if you so desire.

Could any of these ghosts be the spirit of Matthew Thornton or his son? Maybe it is the wraith of Edward Goldstone Lutwyche coming back to claim the land taken from him in such a discriminatory manner. Maybe it is all of them.

Whoever they are, the spirits are now sharing a new lease on life with the newly renovated building. In 2004, Common Man Hospitality Group, a local food chain, purchased the building and turned it into a restaurant again. The renovations were to bring the house back to its colonial appearance. This is the only one of the five Common Man restaurants in New Hampshire that seems to be haunted. The ghosts were there first, so that *does* carry some weight. Owner Alex Ray has worked very hard to undo past renovations and preserve the early charm of the Thornton abode. It can be assured that the ghosts are more at home now.

The restaurant is located at the corner of Greeley Road and Daniel Webster Highway. 603-429-3463. Take Exit 11 off the Everett Turnpike/ Route 3 onto Daniel Webster Highway and follow to the restaurant.

Tortilla Flat Restaurant

Tortilla Flat is housed in a building that was erected as a private residence in the 1700s. It sounds a little out of place for a south of the border fare to take residence, but you can be assured that the atmosphere and cuisine are out of this world. So are some of the visitors one might encounter there as well.

New England Ghost Project turned Arlene and I onto Tortilla Flat for two reasons. The first reason was that it was a great place to eat while in town. The other was that it was haunted. At first glance, it is obvious that there are additions to the original house. The front section still sports the original door. Once inside, there is a room where Zechariah, one of the original residents, hung himself back in the 1700s. The original fireplace still adorns the landscape of this dining area as do old books on the shelf. Those who know the history of the house have dubbed this area "The Hanging Room."

It seems Zechariah is still hanging around, as his spirit is very active. The staff has come in to find the table settings rearranged and chairs, that were once on the tables, taken down and set up elsewhere. The books on the shelf next to the fireplace are constantly moved about and found strewn around the room. Candles relight themselves after being extinguished. Noises are heard after hours, and figures have been spotted moving about the room through the windows long after the place is vacated.

When Arlene and I visited the restaurant, the staff was exceptionally accommodating. We mentioned our knowledge of the place, and they told us more stories of how items fly off shelves, and that there are supposedly several spirits in the place. It was once a stop for the Underground Railroad. Many slaves were hid in the basement on their torturous journey to freedom. It is no doubt some of them died from the appalling conditions they had to endure along the way.

A *sensitive* visited the restaurant and claimed that the spirits of two children and two women still linger there. One is said to be a slave who probably died in the house. New England Ghost Project has EVP recordings and photos to back up the reported haunting of the building. When Karen Mossey asked if Zechariah was present, he answered, "I'm Here." They had other experiences with the paranormal on their two visits that are available for review on their website, www.negostproject.com.

The original portion of the colonial homestead that is now Tortilla Flat. Door enters into haunted dining area.

I must say, I can relate to their experiences. As I was leaving the bathroom, the door that I was holding open tried to forcefully close itself against me. There was no one else on the other side, as it opened against a wall and into a long corridor. It would appear that one of the ghosts did not care for our questions about the haunting of the place. In the end, Arlene and I felt that Tortilla Flat was a magical place to visit for dinner. The staff was great, the food was awesome, and the spirits were always there to keep things interesting.

Tortilla Flat is located at 595 Daniel Webster Highway, Merrimack, New Hampshire 03054. Take Everett Turnpike to Exit 12, Bedford Road towards Route 3. Turn right onto Bedford Road. Turn right onto Daniel Webster Highway. Tortilla Flat is a few hundred yards down the road after a convenience store.

Fireplace room of original structure where Zechariah reportedly hung himself in the 1700s. Now a dining room, this is where most EVP recordings and ghostly photos are obtained.

Milford

Burns House

This old abandoned house is the home of a phantom child. The little girl is seen in the upstairs window looking eastward. Photographs, supposedly taken by some Milford High School students, reveal the image of the ghostly youngster peering from the window on the second floor. The house has been abandoned for many years. At this point, its status is unknown.

Lorden Plaza

This shopping plaza seems to have a permanent resident in the hardware department of their home improvement store. The manifestation is seen in jeans and a plaid shirt wandering down the aisle before disappearing through some plywood. He is also said to carry a tape measure. The identity of the ghost is unknown. Perhaps it is looking for some old house.

The Lorden Plaza is located at 586 Nashua Street, Milford, New Hampshire 03055. Take Route 3 to Exit 8, Route 101A West, Milford/Amherst. Follow 101A for six and one half miles to the plaza.

Mount Clinton

Mizpah Hut

The Mizpah Hut is located at thirty eight hundred feet above sea level on the southern region of Mount Clinton. It is at the very end of the Presidential Range. The cabin overlooks Crawford Notch, Dry River Wilderness, and Montalban Range. Mizpah means "pillar in the wilderness." The views are absolutely breathtaking. The fact that it is haunted only adds to the adventure waiting at the end of the two and one half hour trek up the mountain to the hut.

The shelter was built in 1965. It is three times the size of the Madison Hut. There are eight bunkrooms with accommodations for up to sixty weary hikers to rest. Mizpah is the second largest of the Appalachian Mountain Club huts along the trail. The hike is moderate but appetite forming so be prepared to set for some mountain vittles, as it is a full-service facility with dinner in the mess hall at 6:00 p.m. sharp. Breakfast is also served at 7:00 a.m. for those who care for overnight stay. Advance reservations are required—it can get pretty full in the summer months.

The solar powered palace on the peak also has an equipment store in case of a failure in a hiker's gear while ascending to the hut. Other amenities include a game room, a self-service kitchen, and a library. The ghosts of Mizpah are also included in the stay.

A child's voice has been heard by guests in the middle of the night calling out for her mother. The serene quiet of the mountain is suddenly broken by the macabre cries that resonate in and around the hut. There are also accounts of an apparition of a little girl seen on the first floor. Most likely, it is the ghost of the girl whose chilling calls emanate throughout the cabin. She is known to appear and disappear at all hours of the night. There is no known record of a girl dying or getting lost in the mountain area of the hut, however. People have traveled the trails since early settlers to the White Mountain region, so it is anybody's guess regarding the identity of the phantom child.

The Mizpah Hut can be reached by Crawford Path. Take Interstate Route 93 to Exit 40, Route 302. Follow to the Crawford Notch area and park in the lot for Mount Clinton. The hut is open from May to October, depending on the weather.

Nashua

The Country Tavern

Tragic events and hauntings are no strangers to each other. A dreadful moment can be eternally etched into the place it occurred. The characters involved often linger in that spot forever appearing to us as if trying to reach the world they left so abruptly. The spirits are obviously aware of their surroundings. In the case of the Country Tavern, the spirit is not only aware of her surroundings, but is also interactive with the modern flow of people that come through its doors to dine or quench their thirst at the bar.

The spirit of the Country Tavern is Elizabeth Ford. Over two hundred years ago, she married a sea captain. The generous husband built her a beautiful home in Nashua on farmland that was in his family. The year was 1741, and maritime trade was booming. Shortly after their wedding, he set out to sea on a long voyage. About one year had passed before he was able to reunite with his young bride. Upon returning home, he found that she had just given birth to a child.

In a fit of anger and evidently very hurt over her unfaithfulness, the captain murdered Elizabeth, then killed the infant. One account states that he threw Elizabeth's body down the deep well in the back yard and then buried the baby where no one would find it. Another account tells of how he buried both bodies somewhere on the property to cover up his heinous deed. Either way, the captain was never brought to justice. Perhaps he sailed away, never to return. His fate is a matter of conjecture. The fate of Elizabeth, however, is set in stone. She now haunts the very tavern she once called home. Though it is quite different from when she roamed the walls as a living mortal, the building still exudes a colonial charm.

Since it became a restaurant in 1982, hundreds of people have witnessed her ghost. Jon Randall and Camille Lebbos have owned the tavern since 1995, and have many tales to tell. When I spoke with Jon, he was matter-of-fact in his manner as if he has told of the ghostly accounts an endless amount of times. I do not doubt that he has had to.

They have witnessed dishes fly off the shelf, coffee cups rise and hurl themselves across the room, and even food has taken on ethereal wings. According to a psychic that once held a séance there, Elizabeth was not aware that her home was now a restaurant, and was very upset over so many people invading her privacy.

Bonnie Gamache has worked at the tavern since it opened in 1982. One of the first meals she served, ended up on the floor. Elizabeth flung both plates off the table in front of the wide-eyed, hungry customers. Needless to say, they made haste for the exit. Witnesses have seen Elizabeth on numerous occasions as well. She is described as a beautiful woman wearing a long white dress laced with blue ribbon. Some have seen her at the window of the large dining room that was once a barn, while others have seen her standing in the doorway near the other dining room. Why she still makes an appearance is anybody's guess. She has been made aware that her home is now a "Victual Tavern" and seems to be okay with the idea. She likes to play pranks on the staff and patrons of the restaurant, or turn the radio up suddenly and flick the lights on and off. She will open doors at will or be heard walking around upstairs. She has even been known to play with customers' hair. One waitress had salad dressing lifted from her tray and dumped all over the front of her shirt. It seems Elizabeth could be a bit rough at times, as well.

The Country Tavern, where the ghost of Elizabeth Ford still greets guests.

Jon Randall says that he has never seen Elizabeth to date, but does not scoff at the countless witnesses who have had the honor (of sorts) to experience Elizabeth Ford's presence. He is so busy preparing to give his customers a dining experience that they will long remember, a train could pass through the kitchen and he might not notice. Even during our conversation, he was quite friendly, but totally attuned to his cuisine artistry that has made every customer of the tavern a patron for life.

Who knows? Maybe the person he saw out of the corner of his eye one night was not a chef. Perhaps the woman he spied gliding through the hall was not a customer looking for the restroom.

Maybe Elizabeth will one day tap him on the shoulder and assure him that he is doing a superior job in his pursuit of creating one of the finest dining environments that a person can experience—both living, or otherwise.

The Country Tavern is located at 452 Amherst Street, Route 101A, Nashua, New Hampshire 03063. 603-889-5871. Take Exit 8 off the Everett Turnpike. Bear right at the third set of lights onto Amherst Street. Take a left at the second set of lights into the parking lot at the rear of the building.

Table and booth, where Elizabeth's spirit frequents the most.

Indian Rock Road—The Terrified Child

Tales abound of dark roads where evil lurks among the trees, waiting for unsuspecting victims to wander by. Many of these tales are born of frightened young people traversing these thoroughfares in the dead of the witching hour. The scenery has some landmarks, such as burial grounds or abandoned homes that bear the creation of folklore. Some are born of actual tragedies that have left their mark on the area to replay over and over again. Others are a mix of both. In the case of Indian Rock Road, it could be the latter.

It is rumored that a house once existed on the road next to a cemetery. Someone broke into the house and killed the family. The youngest son of the family managed to escape the bloody massacre and flee towards the street. He did not get far. The young boy was shot in the back as he ran out into the road to flag down a motorist for help.

Many travelers of the road have witnessed the phantom boy on the side of the road. Motorists have locked up their brakes in order to avoid hitting a child that just bolted out into their path. The panicked driver then looks around to find the boy, only to recollect that there was no thud or thump from an impact. There is also no sign of a boy. That is when they realize they have just encountered the phantom child of Indian Rock Road. They also get a feeling of being watched from the woods, and feel sudden cold spots follow them.

The section of road where the ghost appears is layered with skid marks from automobiles locking up in order to avoid the wraith. Some get out to look for the boy. Some know better.

Indian Rock Road also spans into Hollis near the Pine Hill Cemetery. There is a story that relates how the Blood family in Pine Hill Cemetery were killed and now haunt the area, but as you read about the Pine Hill Cemetery in Hollis, you will see that perhaps some of the accounts of *this* story and *that* one were jumbled over time. This might help to set the record straight. As for the ghost of Indian Rock Road, let the tire marks be your guide.

Indian Rock Road is in the northwestern section of Nashua and runs into Hollis.

Take the Everett Turnpike to Exit 6 and follow Pine Hill Road West for about two miles to Indian Rock Road. Take a right onto Indian Rock Road.

Indian Rock Road, where the wraith of a child runs out in front of automobiles.

Gilson Road Cemetery

Gilson Road Cemetery is said to be one of the most active, if not the most active, cemetery in New Hampshire. This is not due to the number of interments, but rather the already interred. Paranormal investigators say that the activity had dwindled, for a time, when a neighborhood was erected across the street. But once again, the graveyard is becoming more and more active with the passing of time.

The cemetery was reported to have a ghost at every stone. Psychics come to Gilson Road to experience the strong energy that the graveyard emits. There are a lot of residual haunts and EMF meters have flown "off the charts" in this holy resting ground. (An EMF meter is a device that measures electro-magnetic frequency. These frequencies are everywhere and register at different strengths. When a haunting is present, the meter, which may have been dormant moments before, will jump and begin to read the presence of something. Electro-magnetic interference and spirit activity go hand in hand. If you do not have an EMF meter, a plain compass will do. The needle is magnetic and will point towards Magnetic North until spirit energy sends it spinning in the direction of the phenomena.)

Misty figures have been seen and photographed moving among the stones. Voices have also been heard within the walls of the burial ground. Many witnesses have reported seeing a hooded figure standing at the far wall of the cemetery. Animals have been known to mysteriously shy away from the walls of the graveyard. Karen Mossey of The New England Ghost Project has gotten numerous EVP recordings at the graveyard and even pictures of orbs and figures. You can check out their investigations or contact them through www.neghostproject.com for more information.

Ghost Quest from New Hampshire got much of the same phenomena. They also felt the presence of a woman and child there. They have strange EVP recordings and photographs as well. You can see their investigations at www.ghostquest.org.

Arlene and I parked the car across the street where it is said that something prevents people from crossing the road to the cemetery. We were so excited to start our investigation, that a bulldozer would not have kept us back. There is a sign on the outside of the wall stating that any unlawful acts to the cemetery are punishable by seven years imprisonment and a $10,000 fine. (After seeing how many burial grounds are disrespectfully treated, we feel that every cemetery should be posted in such a manner and vigorously enforced.) We snapped many pictures and took some EVP recordings. All seemed peaceful until the compass needle began to sway to and fro. At that point, we no longer felt as if we were alone in the cemetery. It was indisputably crackling to life. The EMF meter I had placed on a rock began to chatter. We took pictures in the vicinity of the gauge. Maybe it was just the camera, but a reddish image was visible when the film was developed. We also got what sounds like an EVP, but it is very faint and hard to recognize—so it is left up to conjecture.

A view of Gilson Road Cemetery. Note areas behind stones where there are burials but no markers.

One other point of mention is that one of the Gilson stones had a hole in it that was actually drilled through. We wondered if perhaps it might have been a heavy shingle of some sort converted into a burial marker, or maybe a drill hole from when the stone was being quarried. Farmers were not as wealthy nor did they have access like we do today to many items. Many of the rural folk had to make due with what was available at the time. We have seen countless historical cemeteries where there are numerous unmarked stones. The family would place the temporary marker in the place of the grave until they could either afford to procure a proper stone, or get to a stone maker. More often than not, they never got to do either.

Gilson family stone with hole drilled in it. Perhaps taken from a slate roof or part of a quarry stone.

The area was the site of numerous Native American tribal wars in the seventeenth century. Many a brave warrior was left for dead and rotted away on the grounds that are now the cemetery. This could be why it is so active with paranormal phenomena. Sensitive people even claim that an eerie energy force emerges from the woods around noon each day. They have felt the bizarre power from beyond bear down on them from the trees at the far end of the graveyard.

There are several unmarked graves adding to the mystery of this haunted place. Perhaps many of the ghosts are the souls of those whose graves and names are long forgotten. Their entities now wander around, hoping to regain some eternal recognition.

Gilson Road Cemetery is located on Gilson Road in Nashua. Take Exit 5 West off Route 3, Everett Turnpike. Follow Main Dunstable Road for about two miles. Turn right onto Gilson Road. The cemetery is about one-third of a mile on the right.

Looking through the gates of Gilson Road Cemetery.

New London

Colby-Sawyer College

Almost every college in New Hampshire is haunted. This is not just my opinion, but almost everyone I conversed with on the subject held the same ground. Colby-Sawyer College is no exception. In fact, there are a few buildings that house remnants of the past still roaming the campus for one reason or another. Lets take a quick tour of the haunted places; but first, a short history of the institution's creation.

The college was founded in 1837. It was called an academy back then. It became an institution of higher education in 1928, merging both liberal and professional arts within its curriculum. One of the first buildings on the haunted tour of the college is the Old Academy. This building was erected in 1938, but tragically burned down on April 13, 1992. It was rebuilt, and is now property of the town for their municipal offices. Although the college has left the building, *someone* has not. Footsteps are heard in the empty halls. Running water is heard, even though all faucets are off, and voices permeate the air where no human is there to initiate them. Employees of the building seem to think it is a member of the Colby family, for which the college is named.

The next stop is the library. An unseen ghost likes to rearrange history books and shuffle through pages. Unsuspecting visitors get the shock of their lives as books on tables spark to life with no visible hand to be seen, and pages ramble to and fro. It may have been a history professor, student, or maybe even a past librarian taking a moment to peruse the possessions in this abode of archives.

Another quick stop brings us to the Colby Dorm. Residents have to persevere with ghostly footsteps at night and the rattling of their doorknobs. When they open the door to see who might be trying to enter, they encounter an empty hallway. There are also gusts of wind that blow through the rooms even when the doors and windows are sealed tight. Cold spots follow students around their chambers as well.

Last stop on the tour is the Colgate Building. This is the most active and documented structure, by far, on campus. Money for the hall was funded by Susan Colby-Colgate, with Miss Mary Colgate as representative in 1911. It was dedicated in June of 1912. Apparently someone else who may have had something to do with the building is still making his presence known. A dark figure with a hat and cloak is seen leaning over the railing of the tower on the roof of the hall. Sometimes, he is seen walking along the perimeter of the structure. He then vanishes with no warning.

Fiona Bloome of www.hollowhill.com had first hand experiences with the mysterious ghost while a student at the college. Once in her dorm, she saw the phantom stranger and knew it was a ghost by his appearance. Another time, she saw him while crossing the quadrangle. It was one of the first times in her soon to be illustrious paranormal career that she had encountered a full-figure manifestation. Both times she set out after the specter, but was disappointed when it vanished before she could get close to it. Most people would have turned and made quick distance between the spirit and themselves. Good for you Fiona!

Although she was not fortunate enough to make contact with the eerie entity, that does not mean someone else won't. It could even be *you* if you're lucky—or unlucky, depending on which way you feel about it.

Colby-Sawyer College is located at 641 Main Street, New London, New Hampshire 03257. Take Interstate Route 93 to Route 89 North. Take Exit 11 and follow the signs to New London and the college.

North Salem

Who is Responsible for Mystery Hill?

Deep in the woods of North Salem, New Hampshire off Haverhill Road, just north of the Massachusetts border, lies one of the greatest mysteries and archaeological sites in all of North America. In a seemingly unlikely spot lies what is known as "Mystery Hill" to some, or "America's Stonehenge" to others.

No one really knows who built the ancient village/astronomical calendar. The walls of stone surrounding the structure have specially-placed standing stones to observe celestial events such as the Winter and Summer Solstice, lunar alignments, and other calendar dates of seasonal interest. Around 1500 BC, the Summer Solstice Sunrise Stone was erected within the circle. A notch was cut in the top peak of the stone where the sun could be observed rising on the longest day of the year. The Winter Solstice Sunset Stone has a notch in it as well. Over the years, the earth's rotation has shifted and the sights are off slightly, but scientists have calculated the planet's movement with time, and have concluded that both stones were accurate in their undertaking at the same time about 3,500 years ago. The Spring and Fall Equinox Stone still accurately predicts the turning of the seasons. There is even a stone which lines up the 18.61-year cycle of the moon. At the end of this cycle, the moon appears to have stopped moving. This phenomenon is referred to as the *standstill of the moon*.

The infra-structure of this twenty-acre parcel of land is a primitive complex consisting of twenty chambers, drainage systems, a sacrificial stone with a drain carved in it to catch blood, a speaking tube, and other interesting artifacts of some long-gone civilization. There were a few carvings found in rocks that resemble those of the ancient Phoenicians, but many scholars suggest that Culdee Monks from Ireland actually erected the site. Whoever built the Neolithic calendar did their work about 4,000 years ago.

A chamber now called "Tomb of Lost Souls" is on a perfect east-west axis. This was probably for someone to chart the rising and setting of the sun for purposes of the village's daily routine—much like a rooster crows at dawn and the crickets begin their songs after dusk. The sacrificial stone alone weighs in at four and one half tons. This is attached to a structure called the "Oracle Chamber," which has a rock tube running from inside to under the stone. It is thought that the speaking tube was used during a sacrifice to create the illusion of an omnipresence speaking from the void. A priest would crouch in a small area of the chamber and then astound the unaware flock with his hollow resonant voice. We tried it and it certainly had a manipulating effect as our words spewed from the bottom of the stone into the hollowness of the mountain air. The drainage work cut into the stones seems rather sophisticated for such a primitive time, but is fully functional even to this day. There is so much to see on the self-guided tour of the place, that you just have to witness it for yourself.

The earliest written data of the site goes back to the beginning of the nineteenth century when Johnathon Pattie built a house on the premises. He lived there from 1823 to 1843. The house burned down in 1855. During that time, he sold much of the stonework to the town of Lawrence, Massachusetts for curbstones. At the time, people thought that Indians were responsible for the structure. It wasn't until 1936, when William Goodwin purchased the land for archaeological research to determine who really built the oddity, did its real purpose come to light.

In 1958, America's Stonehenge was opened to the public. My wife and I have paid a few visits to the site and found it to be a magnificent feat of archeological interest. The site is also known for paranormal activity. Strange lights and shapes have been witnessed at the site. Those who claim to be sensitive report an energy field supposedly left behind by the mysterious people who built the megalithic structure. Countless visitors have photographed orbs and strange light forms while touring the attraction.

Research still goes on at the hill to determine, once and for all, who the original builders were. Carbon dating of artifacts and the stone carvings have given researchers clues as to who was there, but all are still too vague to pin the construction down to one race. Perhaps, like England's Stonehenge, it was built over a period of many years by different groups of people. Until we find something extraordinary at the site of Mystery Hill, the delightful attraction will remain, well, a mystery to all.

America's Stonehenge is located at 105 Haverhill Road, P. O. Box 84, North Salem, New Hampshire 03073. 603-893-8300. Take Interstate Route 93 to Exit 3. Follow Route 111 East for 4.5 miles. Watch for the sign to the site. At next traffic light, take a right. Follow for one mile and the entrance is on the right.

Sacrificial stone with blood groove aside the Oracle Chamber.

A view of some of the chambers and ruins of Mystery Hill.

Peterborough

MacDowell Colony

Peterborough is the home of enlightenment. It is no wonder that the first free library in the United States was established here in 1833. In 1907, composer Edward MacDowell and his wife, Marian, expanded on that idea of intellectual stimulation by starting the first artist colony in America. They were well aware that artists of all disciplines enriched each other. They originally purchased their farm in 1896 because Edward found that the parcel of land excelled his creativity.

Somewhere between then and 1906, they realized that this magical breadth of acreage could do the same for others, and set about creating a colony for artists of all walks to congregate and grow both creatively and spiritually. Apparently, a few grew spiritually enough to linger on long after their time.

The colony was founded with the help of Grover Cleveland, Andrew Carnegie, and J. Pierpoint Morgan who started a fund in 1906. One year later, artists began moving in and a dream was realized.

Edward MacDowell died in 1908, but his wife, Marian, expanded and ran the settlement until her death in 1956. More than 5,500 men and women have lived and cultivated into great artists of their genre on the 450-acre spread since its inception. According to present director David Macy, the colony is rich with the presence of the great artists who have come and gone over the years. He also says that is to be expected. Signatures on the wooden tablets hung in the thirty-two studios are a testament to that wonder.

As for the ghosts of the colony, people claimed to have seen the spirit of Eleanor Wylie wandering around. Reports of Edward Arlington Robinson have also surfaced at the settlement. I am sure there are many spirits alive and well in such a magical place.

The colony is listed in the Register of Historic Places and is, therefore, a national landmark. That alone is worth the tour. In August, they have their annual open house and arts awards ceremony. Arlene and I have been invited. Being a writer and musician, it seems like one of the best places to be, or even just to visit, in the world. Both this one, and the other.

The MacDowell Colony is located at 100 High Street, Peterborough, New Hampshire 034358. Take the Everett Turnpike to Exit 7, Route 101A. Follow Route 101A as it turns into Route 101. Bear north onto Route 202 and the colony will be to the left. Plan the trip for their annual open house to get the most of the experience.

Plymouth

Plymouth State University

I am surprised that this is the only haunted place I could find in Plymouth. It seems everyone there wants to keep the ghosts to themselves. No matter. At least there is a habitation of higher learning in Plymouth, and, as usual, it is haunted.

Residence halls seem to house the most ghosts. Mary Lyon Hall once housed the campus kitchen, gymnasium, and area for one of the favorite pastimes of the early twentieth century, a two-lane bowling alley. When it was built in 1916, it was designated as a dorm for women only, but has since gone co-ed. The two white pillars at the entrance look rather intimidating, but it is what's inside that makes the hair on one's neck reach for the heavens.

A malicious female ghost haunts the basement level. Some think it is Mary Lyon herself, still keeping tabs on her namesake. Students are known to take on a fearful side in the basement, as a negative energy suddenly saturates them. It is at that point they forget their duties and make haste for safer havens.

Samuel Read Hall seems to have eyes that follow students around. Residents claim to have feelings of never being alone in their rooms. The gender of the spirit remains a mystery, but the presence remains nonetheless.

Blair Residence was built in the 1960s, but still had time to acquire a male spirit that roams within its walls. Some say it is the lover of Mary Lyon, come back to claim his sweetheart. Someone should tell him he is in the wrong building.

As of this writing, the Mary Lyon Hall and the Samuel Read Hall are undergoing extensive renovations and are expected to reopen in the fall of 2007. I am confident that the ghosts will still be present, and probably more active in the newer walls of the residences. They might even bring a few other unseen friends along to show off their new pads. That is one of the mysteries of the spirit world. You never know who is going to pop up out of nowhere.

Plymouth State University is located at 17 High Street, Plymouth, New Hampshire 03264. Take Interstate Route 93 to exit 25. Take a right at the end of the ramp. At the three-way stop sign, bear left onto Main Street. Take a right at the Post Office, and Plymouth State University Admissions is up the hill on the left at the Russell House.

Portsmouth

The Chase Home

The Chase Home in Portsmouth is haunted. Yet it is also *not* haunted. Now, as you sit there scratching your head wondering what I am talking about, you are feeling the same way I did at first. That is, until I found out there are two houses named after the famous family. Both houses sit in Historical Portsmouth, not too far from each other.

The first Chase Home is part of the Strawberry Banke Museum. Strawberry Banke was the original name for Portsmouth due to the fact that the Indians grew wild strawberries along the shoreline. This is the only museum of its kind where the houses are actually part of the original neighborhood ranging from 1695 to 1950. Unfortunately, our visit to Portsmouth proved all too short to visit the many houses that the museum is comprised of. With all the intense history that lies within the buildings, it would be imprudent to visit Portsmouth and not soak in the early American bonds that helped shape our great nation. The museum is open daily from May to October as a self-guided tour of all the houses—including the not-so-haunted Chase Home.

As I researched the haunted history of the Chase Home, it became very confusing. There were varying accounts of history coinciding with similar years. Either there were two camps regarding the house, one stating the historical side and the other the ethereal side, or there were two completely different homes. As stated before, one belongs to the Strawberry Banke Museum and the other is actually a home for children who stray. I now had to sort out what facts belonged to what house, as I had (like others) previously thought there was only one. The chase was on.

Stacey Brooks, Marketing and Communications Director at the museum, set me straight. The haunted Chase Home is on Middle Street. Many paranormal investigators and psychics have passed through the Strawberry Banke house ranting how it was haunted by a girl who hung herself, and that she still lives there. Then Stacey has to tell them the bad news. Wrong house. Some shy off, quiet and red-faced, while others still swear it is haunted nonetheless.

The "unhaunted" house was built in the nineteenth century and was soon used as a home for children of local sailors. The Chase family graciously minded the children while their fathers were out to sea. Unfortunately, some never returned, and it became apparent that another arrangement was needed for the orphaned offspring.

The haunted Chase Home was built in 1807. Records indicate that railroad magnate and Boston Philanthropist George Chase acquired the building at some point and selflessly donated it to the town for the previously stated use. The home was officially established in 1871. Over the past several decades, it has served as a court appointed home for "wandering children"—as Stacey Brooks put it. The noble intention of the townspeople is truly great, yet even these deeds of goodness and light are blemished with dark moments that have etched themselves into the walls of the interim house.

A young girl is said to have hung herself in her dorm room long ago. Her ghost is now seen in the hallways at night lurking about. Those who see the disturbing apparition approach her apprehensively, until she turns around and runs off into oblivion. Phantom screams emanate from the dorm rooms at all hours of the night, throttling the frightened inhabitants from their slumber. The unfortunate temporary residents must endure these ghostly wails from another world on a steady basis.

The now vacant third floor used to be where the counselors, who tried to help the children in their darkest hours, dwelled. It seems they still reside there in spiritual form. Footsteps and shuffling can be heeded from the rooms above. Fearful ears follow the ghostly footsteps to the top of the stairs leading to the second floor before they trail off into the void.

Even the kitchen staff has had to put up with an unearthly prankster. Lights turn on and off at random. The kitchen fan, with the switch in plain view, will begin its whirling motion at high speed although no one was there to turn it on. Locked doors will be wide open even though the people who own the sole keys to those entrances were not around that day.

So there it is, the two Chase Homes. One home has the history and one has mystery. With all that activity going on in the building, it would seem enough to rehabilitate anyone into wanting to return to their family.

The Chase Home of haunted fame is located on Middle Street in Downtown Portsmouth. Follow the directions for Point of Graves Cemetery, but stay on Middle Street until it becomes Middle Road. The home is on left. Due to security reasons, permission is required to enter the grounds. The Other Chase Home is located in the Strawberry Banke Museum. Follow directions to the Point of Graves Cemetery. The museum is across from the burial ground.

Haunted Chase Home.

The Chase Home that is thought to be haunted, but is not, according to the Strawberry Banke Museum.

John Paul Jones House and Museum

Even if you have never been to Portsmouth, chances are you have seen the John Paul Jones House. Remember those Sears™ paint commercials where they show that beautiful yellow colonial home with the quaint antique windows? That's the place. But it is not what is on the outside walls that is a matter of attention in this book. Instead it is what dwells inside the walls of the homestead that is central to this story.

The house has a rather interesting history. It was around long before the famous paint it sports on its exterior. And it can be assured that the spirits of the interior were there long before as well. The house was built in 1758 as a gift to Sarah Wentworth Purcell from her new husband and sea captain, Gregory Purcell. The house is of Georgian architecture with a gambrel roof and five-bay front. A bay is basically an opening—either a window or door. The interior boasts elegant woodwork carvings and moldings that have been preserved through time.

After the death of her husband, Sarah began taking in boarders to ease the financial burden of the home and her children. American Patriot John Paul Jones (1747 to 1792) was one of those boarders. He was staying there to oversee the final preparations of his ship, *Ranger*. Perhaps he is best known for his famous saying, "I Have Not Yet Begun To Fight." That quote was etched into time as he returned to Portsmouth a Naval hero in 1781. Again, he lodged at the Purcell home. There are rumors through history that he had an affair with Sarah Purcell, but it is not documented, that I know of.

In 1783, Woodbury Langdon, next door neighbor and brother of Governor John Langdon, purchased the house. He apparently lived there while his home next door was being rebuilt after the great fire of 1781. From then on, nine other owners would grace the walls of the Purcell House. Among them included Samuel Lord, Henry and Alexander Ladd, and Senator John F. Parrott.

As the sands of time fell, so did the condition of the house. In 1919, the crumbling relic was given to the Portsmouth Historical Society instead of being demolished. By 1920, the building was restored and opened to the public as Portsmouth's first museum. This is when the ghosts made their regular vigils.

Since then, countless witnesses have seen the face of a woman peering out of the windows of the museum, even when it is locked and secure. She is described as a white-faced specter, staring out of the window through the old-fashioned panes of glass. People of the village seem to think it might be the apparition of widow Purcell looking for her husband, or J. P. J. himself, to return.

There is also a presence residing in the shawl room of the museum. The cabinet door in the room inexplicably flies open whenever someone is present. Several years ago, paranormal investigators conducted a ghost hunt in the museum. They claimed to have encountered the spirit of John Paul Jones in the very room he once slept in. Museum guides have felt the presence of an entity in various rooms at different times. The rear door is known to open and close on its own, prompting the guides to investigate who might be sneaking in the back. They always come up empty handed and puzzled.

Being professional paranormal researchers, as well, Arlene and I wanted to do an investigation of the house; but, unfortunately, it was closed, and our schedule would not allow us to wait until a day when they were open for tours. This time, anyway.

Still, the museum is a perfect example of the historical past of Portsmouth. It is wonderful that such precious items have been preserved for all time. At least the spirits of the house definitely think so.

The John Paul Jones House is located at the corner of Middle and State Streets in Downtown Historical Portsmouth. It is presently home to the Portsmouth Historical Society, 43 Middle Street, P. O. Box 728, Portsmouth, New Hampshire 03802. 603-436-8420. Follow directions for Point of Graves Burial Ground to Middle and State Streets.

The haunted John Paul Jones House and Museum.

Point of Graves Burial Ground

As the waning sun cast long shadows from the graves across the snow, Arlene and I realized that the impending darkness would hasten our visit to Point of Graves Burial Ground. We did not feel so bad about our miscalculation of time, though, because the cemetery, although quite mesmerizing, was very diminutive in size. What disappointed us was the fact that we had too short a spell to soak in the atmosphere and history the stones themselves silently narrated. And, of course, to witness the ghostly phenomena.

Point of Graves was the first common burial ground in the seaside town of Portsmouth. It was deeded to the town in 1671, by Joseph Pickering II, to be used exclusively as a graveyard for its residents. There was one stipulation that allowed for his cattle to graze among the graves. As Arlene and I relentlessly collect historical and haunted data throughout beautiful New England, we found this practice to be common among the early settlers. I guess the grazing livestock doubled as groundskeepers and sometimes fertilizers for the colonial graveyard's grassy greens.

After retiring from our ghostly quests for the evening, we returned the next morning to Point of Graves to get a better look at the cemetery and investigate it in a more thorough fashion.

Point of Graves Cemetery.

Our first focus was the Vaughan tomb that is located in the right hand corner of the burial ground. This particular vault is said to glow when photographed on film. Unfortunately, the pictures we took did not show a luminosity when we reviewed them. I'd hoped to have a great piece of paranormal evidence for the readers, but I guess you will have to witness it for yourself.

We entered the cemetery through the old iron turnstile, and at once found ourselves within the inner perimeter of the graveyard. It is within the confines of the interred that people have heard phantom footsteps behind them as they rambled among the graves. Many tourists and residents have reported sounds of being followed by an invisible entity as they've roamed the small graveyard soaking in the history of this wonderful seacoast settlement. I could have dismissed these accounts as tall tales, but the cemetery is wide open and very small. A mouse would find it hard to keep invisible within the walls of Point of Graves.

The artwork on the stones is Early American folk art. The carvings are definitely worth seeing. The earliest grave dates back to 1682. As we walked among the stones we kept a close ear for the ghostly walkers of Point of Graves. I even attempted to get some EVP recordings (see glossary).

I guess the spirits were at rest this day. It was Sunday, come to think of it. The houses on two sides of the cemetery were quiet and peaceful. The streets that abound the other two sides were sparsely traveled. The Vaughan tomb sits alongside a garage, separated by the cemetery wall. It was truly a pleasant surprise to see this burial place. At first, we expected to be wandering around a vast tract of land filled with countless graves. Fortunately, Point of Graves is all within the cast of an eye.

Sometimes, what you perceive and what is real are two different things. That is what makes paranormal investigations so fascinating. Seeing and hearing is truly believing.

Point of Graves is located across from the parking lot of the Strawberry Banke Museum. Take Interstate Route 95 to Exit 7, Market Street towards Historical District and Strawberry Banke Museum. Follow Market Street to Middle Street. Bear left onto Middle Street to State Street. Bear left onto State Street and then right onto Marcy Street. Parking for the Strawberry Banke Museum is right across from Point of Graves Burial Ground.

The Vaughan Tomb in Point of Graves Cemetery. The tomb is said to glow in photographs.

The Musical Hall

As Arlene and I stood behind the back row of The Musical Hall looking down to the stage, an immense feeling of historical wonder rushed through us. Our ears were tuned to the narration of Production Manager Zhana Morris, but our eyes and imaginations were reliving the illustrious history of the hall, with its lavish Victorian interior and ornate balconies. We almost forgot that we were there because the building was reported to be haunted. It is easy to fathom why spirits would want to reside in this majestic theater. But the question is, were they there before the land was a music hall, or are they residual spirits from one of the many other buildings that once graced the very spot that now houses the theater-going spirit?

Perhaps you might be able to shed some light on the identity of the ghost. Read on and help solve a mystery most unearthly.

The present music hall was built in 1878 on the remains of the previous hall that burned down in the great fire of 1876. The original hall was built as a temple of worship where spiritual programs were held. As the nineteenth century bore on, it became more of a secular place of performance. That was just before the great fire. If we trace the history of the land as far back as possible, we find that it was originally a pasture for the Puritan Ministry to help fund the church. In 1716, the town erected the country's first almshouse. Many a poor citizen was housed there, and it can be assured that numerous died within that hovel.

By 1755, the town saw better use in the structure as a jail. What is now Chestnut Street, was once called Prison Lane. The first of Portsmouth's "Great Fires" broke out in 1781 in the Treadwell family barn. This fire consumed the jail, among other buildings, in the town. A strange fact to note is that there were four such fires between 1781 and 1876 in that area. All of them took place on Christmas according to sources.

By 1806, the site was now the "Temple" as previously mentioned. The only other missing link in the ghostly puzzle is that the site is mentioned in colonial literature as a "Negro" burying ground. Some say that this cemetery extends underneath the present-day Music Hall. So who is the ghost that haunts the theater?

The Portsmouth Musical Hall.

Some say it is a stage hand from a bygone era, still wandering around, as curtains are known to ripple as if someone is walking along the other side of them. The witness will follow the curtain wave to the edge, yet no visible being emerges from the other side. Many people have heard noises and shuffling around in the lobby near the box of-fice. One local even reported to us that she once saw a figure dressed in nineteenth century garb, standing at the stairs when she went out for refreshments. At first, she thought it was an actor or worker creating an ambiance for the audience. When she went to remark on how success-ful the character idea was, the "actor" faded away into thin air. Patrons have also witnessed a dark shadow walk in front of them as they attempt to view the stage. The bizarre shadow moves and dissipates in front of the startled audience member. No one can pin down the identity of the ghost or ghosts that still reside in The Music Hall. Most have found the ghost fascinating and return in hopes of another encounter. For more of the factual history on the hall, there is a book for sale in the lobby that is well worth reading.

Whether you are there for the spirit of the show or the spirit of the the-ater, it does not matter. Everyone who comes to see a performance never leaves disappointed. But sooner or later, *most* of them do leave.

The Music Hall is located at 28 Chestnut Street, Portsmouth, New Hampshire 03801. 603-433-3100. Follow directions to Point of Graves Burial Ground but stop at the Rockingham Hotel. The Music Hall is actu-ally right behind the hotel.

Looking for ghosts in the otherwise empty hall.

The Rockingham Hotel

While sitting in the Library Restaurant of the Rockingham Hotel, we reflected on our days work of searching and reviewing all the haunted places in the area. The guides were courteous and the interviews sincere. But we were not exactly finished with our ghost hunts for the day. That is why we entered the Rockingham in the first place. You guessed it. The place is haunted. It seemed like the fitting place to end the day with dinner and perhaps a spirit or two wandering by.

The majestic brick edifice sits next to the John Paul Jones Museum at the very beginning of State Street from Middle Street. There is no missing the stately hotel-turned-apartments, with its name strewn across the front in great gold letters and the magnificent golden lions waiting to greet you at the top of the granite steps, coercing you into the building. It kind of looks out of place in the midst of all the eighteenth and nineteenth century wooden-sided homes. Yet it is fully among its peers in the circles of the haunted in the area.

Originally, the building was a smaller residence built by Woodbury Langdon, Revolutionary War judge, and older brother of famous New Hampshire Governor John Langdon. The great fire of 1781 destroyed the home along with many others, when the blaze started in a barn that is near the present-day music hall behind the hotel. (See The Music Hall.)

Langdon rebuilt the house in 1785, and resided there until his death in 1805. From there, it became a public house, and in 1884, successful brewer Frank Jones purchased the building and enlarged it into a grand hotel. Luck did not seem to be with the building, though, as another fire damaged the structure in 1884. Prompt work and diligence returned the Rockingham Hotel back to the elegance that people can see to this day.

It later became apartments and then condos in 1973, but somewhere along its lavish history, it picked up a permanent tenant—that of a female ghost who walks the walls of the Rockingham. Today, fine citizens and tourists alike rub elbows at the bar of the restaurant, or dine within the large room that once served as the library. The hotel staff even presents your check slid within the pages of one of the many antique books that grace the walls of the establishment. Maybe one of those books might hold the real clue as to who the ghost of the Rockingham truly is.

The roaming phantom is thought to be that of Woodbury Langdon's wife, who was rumored to have had an affair with John Paul Jones. Jones boarded next door at the Purcell house that now bears his name. Maybe she still roams the halls and rooms of the public house trying to clear her name.

Some say the ghost was a guest at the hotel who tragically drowned at the seashore that is but a few blocks from the hospice. Witnesses say she appears in a white dress, and her presence is forewarned by the strong smell of the sea. Either way, when the pungent odor of the salty brine fills your olfactory senses at the Rockingham, you know that you are about to have an eerie encounter with the wraith in white.

Esther Buffin, Portsmouth's first elected official poet, penned a verse about the lady in white at the Rockingham after she witnessed the spirit in her apartment while residing there.

Who *is* the white lady ghost? As we sat there in the restaurant, we hoped maybe she would wander by so we could perhaps ask. The two lions at the top of the stairs at the building's entrance might hold the answer to the lady in white. They obviously have not come forth, though, and it can be assumed in this case that this is a good thing.

The Rockingham Hotel is on State Street. Follow directions to Point of Graves Burial Ground. The hotel is on your left, as soon as you enter State Street.

The Rockingham Hotel.

Sheafe Street Inn

This nineteenth century building lived its whole life as a tavern and inn. The now empty structure sits on the corner of Sheafe Street and Penhallow Street in Portsmouth's Historical District. The inn has been associated with some very strange tales since its creation.

One of the owners retained her bedroom on the first floor of the inn where the breakfast chamber later sat. One night, she entered the room and proceeded to ready herself for a good night's rest. Some unknown entity had other plans. As she sat on the bed to remove her day clothes, she was immediately thrown to the floor by a brute force. This frightened her so much that she sprang from the room and stayed the night at her neighbor's. The next morning, all was quiet within the inn.

It is also reported that sailors walking by the building would find themselves in a tangle with the invisible bully. They would be inexplicably thrown to the sidewalk before they could even blink an eye. Witnesses said it felt like something jumped out of a window from above onto them.

A man staying at the inn once saw a phantom hunter and his spirit canines walking behind him as he left the Sheafe Street Inn. At first, he heard a low whistling sound and then the yips of dogs. When he turned around, there was the bizarre apparition moving towards him. Years later, five other people witnessed the ghost dressed as a horseman. This seemed strange at first, but later equestrian gear was found in one of the walls during a renovation.

Another spirit that haunts the inn seems to have an obsession against alcohol in the rooms. Famous carver of eagles, John Haley Bellamy, passed away at the inn on April 6, 1914. He is said to be the spirit that smashes the decanters of liquor brought into the rooms by guests. Perhaps he had a change of spirit about spirits in the afterlife. He is also blamed for opening windows to the rooms when they are vacant.

Although they have pinned the blame on Bellamy's ghost for the ghoulish goings on in the rooms, no one has a clue as to who the phantom gourmet in the bakery is. The one-floor bakery is attached to the inn and shares, not only a plot on the corner streets, but a few specters as well. Cooks in the bakery constantly get the feeling that there is someone else with them in the kitchen while they are preparing their delicious cuisine. Many of the chefs have also claimed that tools are in disarray when they arrive in the morning. The night before they had cleaned up and put everything in its usual place. The most disturbing occurrence noted by the staff is the utensils that are put out for specific jobs become suddenly and neatly put back in their places. Within seconds!

Either the mysterious ghost does not care for pastry, or is an ethereal neat-nick. I think the latter applies here, but you can visit yourself and draw your own conclusion.

Follow directions for Point of Graves Burial Ground, except take a left onto Sheafe Street from State Street before you reach Marcy Street.

Ye olde haunted Sheafe Street Inn.

The Sise Inn—The Hosts with the Most Ghosts

Downtown Portsmouth is full of beautiful historic buildings. Each one has its own personality to go with its background. It's no wonder that they should have their own ghosts as well. In the case of the Sise Inn, there appears to be several possible entities that are willing to share a room with eager visitors for a night or two. Exactly who the spirits of the Sise Inn are is anybody's guess. Maybe the history and accounts you are about to read might unlock a clue as to who has never left the building. Or as some think, who has entered the antique edifice.

In 1879, wealthy business merchant John Sise purchased the Marsh estate. Sise was involved in a crockery business with his father and brother. He later ran a prosperous insurance business, as well as being director of the Eastern Railroad and Portsmouth Gas, Electric Light and Power Company. He was also a trustee of the Portsmouth Bank and served as a Justice of the Peace and Notary Public. Such prestige in a community like Portsmouth well afforded a grand scale home.

The original building was built in 1798 for Charles Treadwell. The Marsh family occupied it up until Mr. Sise took ownership. John Sise was married to Lucy Marsh, so the estate stayed in the family, so to speak. He immediately built a new Queen Anne-style home on the site, and in 1881, John, Lucy, and their daughter, Mabel, moved into the three-story mansion.

Mabel grew up and married an Antiquarian Minister of the South Church. She and Alfred Gooding assumed ownership of the property after her father's death in 1898 at the age of sixty-eight. The building remained a private residence until the 1930s, when it was converted to offices. At one point, it was a fashion shop, apartments, and even a halfway house for the mentally ill.

In 1986, the mansion was renovated into an inn. The owners added a charming atrium for guests to soak up the sun while relaxing indoors. The thirty-four guest rooms and common rooms of the inn have the original Victorian look of yesteryear, and guests are treated like royalty. No wonder the ghosts do not want to leave.

There are several reported spirits wandering around the inn. Suite 204 seems to be a favorite haunt for some of the ghosts, as well as the ice machine on the third floor. One night, a desk clerk heard the ice machine on the third floor spewing cubes. Since there was no one at the inn that night, it became a matter of investigation. As she neared the machine, she saw a trail of ice leading to room 204. All the doors had been securely locked, except room 204. As she entered, she saw the ice cubes on the floor, but the room was completely void of the living. She was sure that she was alone in the inn, and upon checking the third floor for trespassers, became unnerved over that fact.

The key to room 204 is constantly misplaced. At one point, none of the keys to the room worked. They called in a locksmith who tried the door and it opened with ease. It would appear that something wanted privacy in the room for a while.

Room 204 is not the only place where ghosts reside in the inn, however. One chambermaid reported being pushed into a closet by unseen hands. She recalled later that it felt like a male presence, trying to force her into the closet for some unknown reason. Another employee was tidying up a room when she, all of a sudden, felt hands on her hips. She reeled around in panic, but there was no one behind her. A guest at the inn reported that something entered her room, then lay down on the bed beside her. The alarmed woman could see the bed sag with the imprint of a person, yet there was no visible entity present.

One guest was greeted with a flying plant in a pot. This was enough for the patron to request another chamber for the night. Many people have witnessed the rocking chair next to the main desk start to sway to and fro on its own volition. The elevator also has a mind of its own, as it will start up and stop at different floors, even when the inn is completely vacant. The door will open for a moment then close, as the spectral rider continues on its way.

Who are the spirits that haunt the Sise Inn? There is a lot of speculation. There are rumors that a butler of John Sise had an affair with one of the maids. When she spurned him, he hung himself in what is now room 204. No records pertaining to this account exist, so make of it what you will. Evidence does suggest that the entities might be that of a couple that once lived a few houses over. The man murdered his wife in 1905. Many say that they migrated to the Sise Inn after their home was destroyed.

Whether you believe any of these theories, or just think that the spirits are patrons and residents of the past lingering on, is really up to you. One way you can find out is to spend a night at the haunted inn, and perhaps you, too, can get into the *spirit* of the place.

The Sise Inn is located at 40 Court Street, Portsmouth, New Hampshire 03801. 603-433-1200. Take Interstate Route 95 to Exit 7, Market Street Extension, Portsmouth. Turn right at the end of the ramp. Go through the first set of lights to the blinking light and take a right onto Russell Street. Bear right at the stop sign onto Deer Street to the first set of lights. Take left at the light onto Maplewood Avenue. Go through three sets of lights and take a left onto Court Street. The inn is on the right, with ample parking in the rear of the building.

The Sise Inn, with its numerous spirits to keep guests company.

Ringe

Franklin Pierce College—The Manor

Franklin Pierce was the only New Hampshire citizen to be elected as President of the United States of America. He was the fourteenth individual to hold that prestigious honor, and the youngest at the time. His moniker sat in the waiting list of people who would be named after colleges for a long spell. It was not until November 14, 1962, when Frank DiPietro named his facility of higher education after him, that Mr. Pierce became memorialized. There are some discrepancies over the ordinary history of the parcel of land and the haunted history. Yes, the building that sits there is now claimed to be haunted by a woman who ran a brothel there around the turn of the century, but as you read on, there is no mention of this fact in the historical pamphlets of the school. Let's let you, the reader, sort out this thrilling tale of ambiguity.

There is a building that existed on the property long before the notion of a college was ever derived. In 1854, a sea captain named Asa Brewer lived on the land. He was a passionate fellow, who also used the site as a stopping point for the famous Underground Railroad. In 1902, George Emory, a wealthy importer of mahogany, obtained the land and built a manor and carriage house for his prized horses. In 1924, Arthur Lowe bought the estate and graciously turned it over to the Fitchburg, Massachusetts chapter of the Boy Scouts of America Council. The grassy hill at the base of Mount Monadnock overlooking Pearly Pond was a summer camp for the troops for seventeen years. In 1948, silent movie actress Alma Monaco purchased the estate and lived there until 1962, when she sold it to Mr. DiPietro. None of these details jive with what you are about to read next.

According to other sources, the site was a brothel run by a woman named Edna McGuinness, around the turn of the century. She hung a large portrait of herself on the stairway leading to the second landing. According to legend, when she died, the building was sold, but the portrait was never removed from its spot.

An employee was cleaning the manor in 1990, when she heard the ethereal sound of a piano echoing from the function room. This would not seem so eerie, except that there was no piano in the room, and had not been for many years. The woman searched the manor for a source of the sound, but found that she was alone. As she began to question her imagination, she was halted in her tracks by the most horrific spectacle. Coming down the stairs was the manifestation of a woman carrying a baby. The apparition had a strange glow to it and emitted a humming sound as it descended towards the frightened woman.

Witnesses still experience strange feelings when in the manor, and have reported seeing the ghost of a woman looking out of the second-story window towards Pearly Pond. Could it be Edna McGuinness? Is any of it true? There is no mention of what was there before the manor was built in 1902. Let's leave this one for you to visit and find out for yourself the real truth behind the haunting of the manor. Perhaps the existence of a brothel is a fact that was brushed under the rug to maintain the integrity of the school. Who knows? The spirits are not going to give up information so easily. Good luck on this one.

Franklin Pierce College is located at 20 College Road, Ringe, New Hampshire 03461. Follow Route 202 into Ringe. Take Route 119 West for one and one half miles to the blinking light. Turn onto College Road.

Rye

Ray's Seafood Restaurant

Something fishy is going on at the building that houses Ray's Seafood Restaurant. This popular beachfront eatery boards a permanent resident ghost named "Goldie," who haunts the top floor of the establishment.

The spirit likes to open locked windows and let the brisk, sometimes chilling, ocean air into the rooms. There is a story that is told about the owner's children sneaking down to the bar to slip a few drinks. At that point, the ever-vigilant Goldie is said to have made the phone ring like an alarm to draw the owner into the tavern area. This only startled the young experimenters of the alcoholic nectars quartered behind the bar. Her next attempt was to make all the glasses in the room start shaking and rattling violently. This trick worked, as the youngsters abandoned their mission and fled the lounge in terror.

Not much more is known about the ghost of the restaurant. The food is great and the scenery is everything a person can expect, being next to the sea. Maybe someone should ask the ghost her identity the next time they see her. She *does* make an occasional appearance. Even if you don't get to see the ghost, the experience is worth the trip.

Ray's Seafood Restaurant is located at 1677 Ocean Boulevard, Rye, New Hampshire 03870. Take Interstate Route 95 to Exit 5. Take Route 1 Bypass South. Follow Route 1 South. Take a left onto Elwyn Road at the light. Follow to Route 1A South. Continue past the Science Center, and Ray's is on the right.

Strafford

Bow Lake

Lakes are places of year-round wonder. In the summer, there is the roar of motorboats towing skiers by the crowded beaches, as visitors soak up the sun and water. Then there is the quiet twilight fisherman braving the bugs, hoping to catch the trophy he can boast about for years to come. In the winter, yelps of laughter and marvel come to life on the ice, as skaters of all ages congregate to enjoy the water's new face in the heart of the frosty season. In the case of Bow Lake, there seems to be one more side to this body of water that is not so welcome and appealing to the local throng.

Reports of unearthly screams and moans rise up from the water's depths and permeate the peaceful nighttime air. Cries for help from a disembodied source are most unnerving to visitors and the residents around the lake. There are also reports of bright lights coming from the woods and creepy shadows lurking just beyond the edge of the trees around the lake.

One of the strangest occurrences is, what appears to be, sunshine coming from the area in the middle of the night. Witnesses have pinned the phenomena down to a time near midnight to 3:15 in the morning. The residents have also heard the ghostly voices calling people's names, yet there is no one in sight. There is a campground at the lake and many places to swim or launch a boat, if you dare…

Bow Lake is located in Strafford, with a small piece of it in Northwood. Take Exit 14, Route 9 East off Interstate Route 93. Follow Route 9 into Northwood. Take a left onto Bow Lake Road. Once in Strafford, this becomes Piper Road, then Northwood Road. The road connects with Province Road as it circles the lake.

Stratham

Merrill House

Frying Pan Lane and Bunker Hill Avenue are not only the intersections of two old roads, but a crossroads for the living and the dead as well. The house on the corner of these two thoroughfares has been there for about 300 years. And the ghost of Annie Merrill has been a permanent fixture in the home since 1882.

Seventeen-year-old Annie Merrill became engaged to Frank Berry on December 13, 1878. Sometime between then and October 15, 1881, the relationship went sour, and Mr. Berry ended up marrying Mary S. Jewell. Although Annie wished her former betrothed well, it was obvious that the ordeal had severely broken her heart. Notes found in the eaves of the attic and entries from her diary show that she was quite grief-stricken by the event. The final entry to her diary was in the form of a suicide poem written in 1882. It was sometime after that when Annie, still distraught over being jilted by her lover, hung herself in the woodshed that connected the house and the barn.

The Conery family bought the home in 1953. Their experiences include the constant opening and closing of the door leading from the pantry to the woodshed. Disturbances from an upstairs room kept the family up at night. This was thought to be Annie's room. Animals would approach the stairs, then cower and run. The haunting of the house seemed to grow more intense until the writings were discovered. It seems that Annie Merrill is now more at peace since the telling of her story.

The Merrill House is at the corner of Frying Pan Lane and Bunker Hill Avenue in Stratham. It is a private residence so proper respect should be given. Any explicit directions are omitted for that reason. I only include this in the book as it is a famous New Hampshire haunt and is worthy of further reading.

Suncook

Emerson Mills Apartments

Now an apartment complex, the Emerson Mill was one of several paper mills that graced the Suncook River. One of the mills was suspected of producing paper for counterfeit money. These mills operated from the 1700s into the early 1800s. Most of them were either razed or destroyed by fire. The Webster Mill burned in 1982, leaving the Emerson Mill as the lone survivor of the group. At some point in time, it was converted into an apartment complex.

This mill building, like all others with such history etched into its walls, does not start a new lease on life without some remnants of the past crossing into the present on occasion. The whole building is reported haunted. Paranormal researchers have had great success in the building and have witnessed apparitions as well as feelings of uneasiness. Some have felt a foreboding sense of fear lurking in the complex. There are countless reports of shadow people and the feeling of being watched. If you like ghosts, this is the place to live. If you don't, well most apartments are reputed haunted in some way, so why not pick one rich with history? That way, there is always something to see—or at least *feel* in the building.

Emerson Mills Apartments is located at 100 Main Street in Suncook, New Hampshire 03275. Take Interstate Route 93 to Exit 9 onto Hooksett Road. Bear left onto Pleasant Street. Pleasant Street becomes Main Street once in Suncook.

West Chesterfield

Riverside Motel

Ellen Wood, who manages the Riverside Motel, lives in a section that is both a house and main office at the same time. As I spoke with her about the haunted past at the motel, she appeared to be quite candid and intellectual. Her matter-of-fact parlance assured me that she was not making up what she relayed to me about this place of accommodation.

There was an employee of the motel who would not set foot in one of the rooms, as she was overcome with a dreadful feeling that made her retreat her duties in haste. Ellen agreeably finished cleaning the room, as the staff member would not even go near the door—let alone venture inside. This is not the first time this strange feeling has been documented. There are other reports of people feeling energy in one of the rooms at the motel. Ellen has had her share of encounters as well. On many occasions, she has seen the image of a male wisp by her out of the corner of her eye. Startled and curious, she would get up to investigate. Each search would be in vain, for there was no intruder within her living quarters that she could see. These "Shadow People," as they are called, are a common phenomenon in the spirit world. There are countless cases of people who witness these types of manifestations.

She also recalled how items vanish that were placed down only moments before. Thorough searches turn up empty of the missing object. Then, like some sort of magic, the missing object reappears somewhere else at some point later in time. One time, she was actually touched by a ghost. The spirit of a man touched her on the shoulder, then vanished into oblivion. That was enough to make a believer out of the hardest skeptic.

The identity of this specter is not readily known, but there is a clue as to who he might be. There was a man who committed suicide at the end of the driveway where the Riverside now sits. Perhaps it is his restless spirit looking for peace. The occurrences are not malevolent or disturbing, but they are interesting nonetheless. Book a room at the Riverside Motel, and see if you can ask the ghost who he is. Maybe you can get him to split the room with you for the night. Just make sure he doesn't disappear without paying.

The Riverside Motel is located at 18 Riverside Drive, West Chesterfield, New Hampshire 03466. 603-256-6755. Take Everett Turnpike to Exit 7, Route 101A. Follow until it becomes Route 101 West. Follow into West Chesterfield. Bear onto Route 9 and follow to Golf Road. Take a right onto Golf Road, then a right onto Riverside Road. The motel is up driveway.

Madame Cherri's Staircase

As one is traveling down Golf Road in West Chesterfield, they might catch a glimpse of an odd spectacle. Protruding from the earth is a stone staircase leading towards the sky. No, it is not an apparition, but the misty figure that is seen descending the eerie flight of steps most certainly is. The staircase is all that remains of a castle that was, at one time, a brothel operated by a woman the locals knew as Antionette (Madame) Cherri. This vivacious woman was not shy about her occupation, nor was she reserved when it came to a public display. According to local history, she once trotted down Main Street on horseback stark naked, much to the shock of the townsfolk and the ire of the local authorities.

Antoinette Cherri was born in 1878, and came to West Chesterfield in 1927. She lost her fortune in the depression of 1929 and left the manor to live with a friend. She died in 1965.

At some point, the abandoned brothel met with ill will and burned to the ground. It is said that some people died in the fire. These spirits are frequently reported to return to the scene of their demise. Madame Cherri, however, is witnessed the most as she still tides over her house of pleasure. Some say that there is a cache buried on the property, and that the madam left a stipulation in her will that for the lucky searcher who found it, he or she could keep it.

The staircase is open until dark and then gated for safety reasons, so please obey the rules. The exact nature of the danger that might lurk after dark is not specified, so you can draw your own conclusions.

To get to the staircase, follow directions to the Riverside Motel, but continue on Golf Road for another mile.

Wilton

Vale End Cemetery

There are many witnesses who have documented the supernatural events that take place at Vale End Cemetery. Upon speaking with the people at Vale End, they were not sure if they were *lucky* to experience these occurrences, or not. It seems the ghosts of the graveyard can be truly frightening.

Paranormal investigators have taken photographs of a blue streak that rises from the grave of Mary Ritter and Mary Spaulding. The husband of the two thought it would be a prudent idea to bury his second wife with his first and let them share a headstone. They were both named Mary.

One of them is obviously not happy with the idea. Researchers believe it is Mary Ritter who rises for company to mete out her grievances. The bluish column rises from the grave and stands tall and wide. Some say the grave itself glows, as well. The stone has been studied, and no logical explanation of the phenomena has been brought forth. The grave is on the right hand side of the cemetery in the rear.

Another spirit seen in Vale End is that of an old man. It is said he watches the road, looking for his daughter. Some say he buried his daughter there, and years later, her husband had the grave moved. He is now confused as to where his beloved child is. Others say he watches her as she wanders along the stones, keeping her safer in death than he could in life.

The other ghost of the cemetery is the girl herself. She is said to be the first person interred in the burial ground. It is believed that the ghostly young woman is eternally wandering about the cemetery looking for her grave that was moved by her husband. Investigators and visitors to the eerie necropolis have also claimed to experience cold spots, footsteps from beyond, orbs, and whistling sounds. Documentation in the form of pictures and EVP recordings prove that the cemetery is indeed still alive. There are photographs online for the curious to peruse. I suggest that you would be content with just reading about this place, as the cemetery is heavily patrolled after dark, and those found there between the hours of 7 p.m. and 7 a.m. are subject to some stern trespassing prosecution and fines. This is due to those who have no respect for the dead and have vandalized the stones and grounds of Vale End. It is surprising not more have risen to keep the unwanted out.

Vale End Cemetery is located off of Frye Highway in Wilton, New Hampshire. Out of respect for the cemetery and people of the area, no more information can be disclosed.

Windham

The Windham Restaurant

One of the greatest charms of New England is the many Colonial and Federal era buildings that have been preserved and transformed into bed and breakfasts, inns, museums, or restaurants where the public can indulge in the beautiful architecture or the rigid simplicity of early American life. The atmosphere and restored décor of these antique structures transport visitors back in time when candles and oil lamps flickered, casting a soft glow upon the old milk-paint walls, as a cozy fire was all that was available to warm the chill of the frigid New England winters. The clopping of horse's hooves and the creaking of a chaise was the only distraction one might hear from the world outside.

It is no wonder why so many people from the present day flock to soak in the ambiance of these buildings of yesteryear. It is also no wonder why so many people of yesteryear have stayed behind in them, as well.

The Windham Restaurant is just such a place. The town of Windham is located in Southeastern New Hampshire just over the Massachusetts border. The building that houses the restaurant is one of the oldest and most significant historical sites in Windham. The land was part of a farm that was established in 1729. In 1812, Isaac Dinsmore built a house on it. It was a humble and common home of the time, having a large working room with a massive fireplace and a few smaller rooms upstairs. By the 1820s, the Dinsmore family had expanded the house, adding a mansard roof and two new chimneys. This is what people see to this day as they pull into the Windham Restaurant.

Horace Dinsmore was the next to occupy the home. As a matter of fact, the Dinsmore family kept the home for many generations. Finally, the structure had lived out its tenure as a private home and was converted into a restaurant. At first, it was a Thai restaurant, then it was transformed into a French café called The Riviera. This is when the ghostly activity reportedly began to peak. At the end of 2001, Vess Liakas and his partner, Lula, turned it into the Windham Restaurant. Since then, they have been serving up some of the finest fare one's palate can experience. Patrons of the Windham often have to share their dining experience with a few permanent residents of the building.

One such spirit is that of a little boy who has been witnessed near the second floor waiter station. Diners have also been startled by the appearance of a girl who is spotted wandering around the restaurant. She appears and disappears without notice or warning. There is also a report of a spirit they call "Jacob," who died of a heart attack in the house. It is said that he fell down the stairs after suffering the fatal infliction. The strange part about this story is that one evening, Lula saw a man fall down the stairs. In a frantic moment she ran to help him, but when she reached the bottom of the stairs, the man vanished into thin air.

A waitress was frightened out of the second story dining room one night by an apparition that was sitting in a corner looking at her. When she approached the man to ask why he was still there after the restaurant had closed, the figure faded away in front of her.

Many patrons have reported seeing the spirit of Jacob, who is dressed in blue. No one is really sure who the spirits of the restaurant were in life, but they seem very active and at home in death. Vess told me a lot of accounts and stories about the restaurant from the time before he owned it until very recently while in his possession.

He is the first one in, and the last one out. There are only two keys, and his partner holds the other. On several occasions, he has opened up to find the heavy double windows wide open—even in the dead of winter. It takes two people to open this type of window. One person is needed to help lift the window, and then slide it outward from the frame. He always makes sure they are secure and locked at night. He has heard voices in the restaurant after all the staff have gone home for the night. They have even called his name. On many occasions he has opened the doors in the morning to find the table settings, that were meticulously arranged the night before, strewn about the floor, and chairs pushed out from under the tables. The New England Ghost Project has done several investigations of the building with astonishing results.

Ron Kolek, founder of the organization has witnessed items move, cold spots that suddenly wisp through the dining rooms, and even a necklace unclasp from around the neck of a waitress while he was interviewing her. She stated that such occurrences happen all too often while on duty at the Windham. They seem to love playing pranks on the blonde waitresses more than the others. During one of his investigations, while it still was the Riviera, Ron was witness to a pile of fake Christmas gifts that were under a tree on the second floor suddenly appear in the stairway stretched in mid-air from wall to wall. He was not the only witness to this phenomenon, as the staff was all present downstairs when they heard the commotion. He took photographs of the strange incident.

One evening, he was having dinner at the Windham, when Vess came out to greet him. As they began to talk, both stared in awe as the teapot on the table slide from one side to another. They could only guess the spirits wanted to say hello as well.

Film crews from Channel Four were called in to do a special on the haunted restaurant. (The show will air starting in 2006 at various times.) Vess said that the producers and crew were very astounded by the incidents that have taken place at the Windham. Ron Kolek has stated that the Windham is indeed haunted, and continues to further investigate the ghostly happenings of the building.

Some of the staff are used to the ghosts and their antics, while others still get a chill when the room is suddenly transformed into another place in time, and the spirits begin their tenure for those brief, but memorable moments. Vess puts up with the harmless ghosts of the Windham. They are just going about their business, as well. After all, they were there long before he was, and will be there long after.

The Windham Restaurant is located at 59 Range Road, Windham, New Hampshire 03087. 603-870-9270. Take Interstate Route 93 to Exit 3, then bear right at the end of the ramp. Continue about one hundred feet to the intersection of Route 111 and Route 111A. Turn right and the restaurant is the yellow colonial on the left.

The Windham Restaurant, where the best food and "spirits" in Windham can be found.

Conclusion

There are places you may have read about in the past that are not included in this book. That is because they are either not haunted as told to me by the closest people involved in the aforementioned locations, or they no longer exist. You may also encounter a place or two that has become a memory of the past, between the time of this writing and your acquisition of this tome. That instance is one that I have no control over. Although historic buildings and sites can be preserved, progress tends to eat these places up.

This seems rather strange as we see haunted places as eternal bastions where ghosts can roam their little world forever. It makes us shudder to think that even ghosts of the past can become, ghosts of the past.

Thank you and happy haunting.

* The following section is provided by the Chester County Paranormal Research Society and appears in training materials for new investigators.
Please visit www.ChesterCountyprs.com for more information.

Glossary

Air Probe Thermometer
A thermometer with an external probe that is capable of taking instant measurements of the air temperature.

Anomalous field
A field that can not be explained or ruled out by various possibilities, that can be a representation of spirit or paranormal energy present.

Apparition
A transparent form of a human or animal, a spirit.

Artificial field
A field that is caused by electrical outlets, appliances, etc.

Aural Enhancer
A listening device that enhances or amplifies audio signals. i.e., Orbitor Bionic Ear.

Automatic writing
The act of a spirit guiding a human agent in writing a message that is brought through by the spirit.

Base readings
The readings taken at the start of an investigation and are used as a means of comparing other readings taken later during the course of the investigation.

Demonic Haunting
A haunting that is caused by an inhuman or subhuman energy or spirit.

Dowsing Rods

A pair of L-shaped rods or a single Y-shaped rod, used to detect the presence of what the person using them is trying to find.

Electro-static generator

A device that electrically charges the air often used in paranormal investigations/research as a means to contribute to the materialization of paranormal or spiritual energy.

ELF

Extremely Low Frequency.

ELF Meter/EMF Meter

A device that measures electric and magnetic fields.

EMF

Electro Magnetic Field.

EVP

Electronic Voice Phenomena.

False positive

Something that is being interpreted as paranormal within a picture or video and is, in fact, a natural occurrence or defect of the equipment used.

Gamera

A 35mm film camera connected with a motion detector that is housed in a weather proof container and takes a picture when movement is detected. Made by Silver Creek Industries.

Geiger Counter

A device that measures gamma and x-ray radiation.

Infra Red

An invisible band of radiation at the lower end of the visible light spectrum. With wavelengths from 750 nm to 1 mm, infrared starts at the end of the microwave spectrum and ends at the beginning of visible light. Infrared transmission typically requires an unobstructed line of sight between transmitter and receiver. Widely used in most audio and video remote controls, infrared transmission is also used for wireless connections between computer devices and a variety of detectors.

Intelligent haunting
A haunting of a spirit or other entity that has the ability to interact with the living and do things that can make its presence known.

Milli-gauss
Unit of measurement, measures in 1000th of a gauss and is named for the famous German mathematician, Karl Gauss.

Orbs
Anomalous spherical shapes that appear on video and still photography.

Pendulum
A pointed item that is hung on the end of a string or chain and is used as a means of contacting spirits. An individual will hold the item and let it hang from the finger tips. The individual will ask questions aloud and the pendulum answers by moving.

Poltergeist haunting
A haunting that has two sides, but same kinds of activity in common. Violent outbursts of activity with doors and windows slamming shut, items being thrown across a room and things being knocked off of surfaces. Poltergeist hauntings are usually focused around a specific individual who resides or works at the location of the activity reported, and, in some cases, when the person is not present at the location, activity does not occur. A poltergeist haunting may be the cause of a human agent or spirit/energy that may be present at the location.

Portal
An opening in the realm of the paranormal that is a gateway between one dimension and the next. A passageway for spirits to come and go through. See also Vortex.

Residual haunting
A haunting that is an imprint of an event or person that plays itself out like a loop until the energy that causes it has burned itself out.

Scrying
The act of eliciting information with the use of a pendulum from spirits.

Table Tipping
A form of spirit communication, the act of a table being used as a form of contact. Individuals will sit around a table and lightly place there fingertips on the edge of the table and elicit contact with a spirit. The Spirit will respond by "tipping" or moving the table.

Talking Boards
A board used as a means of communicating with a spirit. Also known as a Quija Board.

Vortex
A place or situation regarded as drawing into its center all that surrounds it.

White Noise
A random noise signal that has the same sound energy level at all frequencies.

Equipment Explanations

I n this section, the Chester County Paranormal Research Society looks at the application and benefits of equipment used on investigations with greater detail. The equipment used for an investigation plays a vital role in the ability to collect objective evidence and helps to determine what *is* and *is not* paranormal activity. But a key point to be made here is: the investigator is the most important tool on any investigation. With that said, let us now take a look at the main pieces of equipment used during an investigation...

The Geiger Counter

The Geiger counter is device that measures radiation. A "Geiger counter" usually contains a metal tube with a thin metal wire along its middle. The space in between them is sealed off and filled with a suitable gas and with the wire at about $+1000$ volts relative to the tube.

An ion or electron penetrating the tube (or an electron knocked out of the wall by X-rays or gamma rays) tears electrons off atoms in the gas. Because of the high positive voltage of the central wire, those electrons are then attracted to it. They gain energy that collide with atoms and release more electrons, until the process snowballs into an "avalanche", producing an easily detectable pulse of current. With a suitable filling gas, the flow of electricity stops by itself, or else the electrical circuitry can help stop it.

The instrument was called a "counter" because every particle passing it produced an identical pulse, allowing particles to be counted, usually electronically. But it did not tell anything about their identity or energy, except that they must have sufficient energy to penetrate the walls of the counter.

The Geiger counter is used in paranormal research to measure the background radiation at a location. The working theory in this field is that paranormal activity can effect the background radiation. In some cases, it will increase the radiation levels and in other cases it will decrease the levels.

Digital and 35mm Film Cameras

The camera is an imperative piece of equipment that enabled us to gather objective evidence during a case. Some of the best evidence presented from cases of paranormal activity over the years has been because of photographs taken. If you own your own digital camera or 35mm film camera, you need to be fully aware of what the cameras abilities and limitations are. Digital cameras have been at the center of great debate in the field of paranormal research over the years.

The earlier incarnations of digital cameras were full of inherent problems and notorious for creating "false positive" pictures. A "false positive" picture is a picture that has anomalous elements within the picture that are the result of a camera defect or other natural occurrence. There are many pictures scattered about the internet that claim to be of true paranormal activity, but in fact they are "false positives." Orbs, defined as anomalous paranormal energy that can show up as balls of light or streaks in still photography or video, are the most controversial pictures of paranormal energy in the field. There are so many theories (good and bad) about the origin of orbs and what they are. Every picture in the CCPRS collection that has an orb—or orbs—are not presented in a way that state that they are absolutely paranormal of nature. I have yet to capture an orb photo that made me feel certain that in fact it is of a paranormal nature.

If you use your own camera, understand that your camera is vital. I encourage all members who own their own cameras to do research on the make and model of the camera and see what other consumers are saying about them. Does the manufacturer give any info regarding possible defects or design flaws with that particular model? Understanding your camera will help to rule out the possibility of interpreting a "false positive" for an authentic picture of paranormal activity.

Video Cameras

The video camera is also a fundamental tool in the investigation as another way for collecting objective evidence that can support the proof of paranormal activity. The video camera can be used in various ways during the investigation. It can be set on a tripod and left in a location where paranormal activity has been reported. It can also be used as a hand-held camera and the investigator will take it with them during their walk through investigation as a means of documenting to hopefully capture anomalous activity on tape. Infra-Red technology has become a feature on most consumer level video cameras and depending on the manufacturer can be called "night shot" or "night alive." What this technology does is allow us to use the camera in zero light. Most cameras with this feature will add a green tint or haze to the camera when it is being used in this mode. A video camera with this ability holds great appeal to the paranormal investigator.

EMF/ELF Meters

EMF = Electro Magnetic Frequency

ELF = Extremely Low Frequency

What is an EMF/ELF meter? Good question. The EMF/ELF meter is a meter that measures Electric and Magnetic fields in an AC or DC current field. It measures in a unit of measurement called "milli-gauss," named for the famous German mathematician, Karl Gauss. Most meters will measure in a range of 1-5 or 1-10 milli-gauss. The reason that EMF meters are used in paranormal research is because of the theory that a spirit or paranormal energy can add to the energy field when it is materializing or is present in a location. The theory says that, typically, an energy that measures between 3-7 milli-gauss may be of a paranormal origin. This doesn't mean that an artificial field can't also measure within this range. That is why we take base readings and make maps notating where artificial fields occur. The artificial fields are a direct result of electricity, i.e. wiring, appliances, light switches, electrical outlets, circuit breakers, high voltage power lines, sub-stations, etc.

The Earth emits a naturally occurring magnetic field all around us and has an effect on paranormal activity. Geo-magnetic storm activity can also have a great influence on paranormal activity. For more information on this kind of phenomena visit: www. noaa.sec.com.

There are many different types of EMF meters; and each one, although it measures with the same unit of measurement, may react differently. An EMF meter can range from anywhere to $12.00 to $1,000.00 or more depending on the quality and features that it has. Most meters are measuring the AC (alternating current, the type of fields created by man-made electricity) fields and some can measure DC (direct current-naturally occurring fields, batteries also fall into the category of DC) fields. The benefit of having a meter that can measure DC fields is that they will automatically filter out the artificial fields created by AC fields and can pick up more naturally occurring electro magnetic fields. Some of the higher-tech EMF meters are so sensitive that they can pick up the fields generated by living beings. The EMF meter was originally designed to measure the earth's magnetic fields and also to measure the fields created by electrical an artificial means.

There have been various studies over the years about the long term effects of individuals living in or near high fields. There has been much controversy as to whether or not long term exposure to high fields can lead to cancer. It has been proven though that no matter what, long term exposure to high fields can be harmful to your health. The ability to locate these high fields within a private residence or business is vital to the investigation. We may offer suggestions to the client as to possible solutions for dealing with high fields. The wiring in a home or business can greatly affect the possibility of high fields. If the wiring is old and/or not shielded correctly, it can emit high fields that may affect the ability to correctly notate any anomalous fields that may be present.

Audio Recording Equipment

Audio recording equipment is used for conducting EVP (Electronic Voice Phenomena) research and experiments. What is an EVP? An EVP is a phenomenon where paranormal voices or sounds can be captured with audio recording devices. The theory is that the activity will imprint directly onto the device or tape, but has not been proven to be an absolute fact. The use of an external microphone is essential when conducting EVP experiments with analog recording equipment. The internal microphone on an analog tape recorder can pick up the background noise of the working parts within the tape recorder and can taint the evidence as a whole. Most digital recorders are quiet enough to use the internal microphone, but as a general rule of thumb, we do not use them. An external microphone will be used always. Another theory about EVP research is that an authentic EVP will happen within the range 250-400hz. This is a lower frequency range and isn't easily heard by the human ear, and the human voice does not emit in this range. EVP is rarely heard at the moment it happens—it is usually revealed during the playback and analysis portion of the investigation.

Thermometers

The use of a thermometer in an investigation goes without saying. This is how we monitor the temperature changes during the course of an investigation. CCPRS is currently using Digital thermometers with remote sensors as a way to set up a perimeter and to notate any changes in a stationary location of an investigation. The Air-probe thermometer can take "real time" readings that are instantly accurate. This is the more appropriate thermometer for measuring air temperature and "cold spots" that may be caused by the presence of paranormal phenomena. The IR Non-contact thermometer is the most misused thermometer in the field of paranormal research. CCPRS does not own or use IR Non-contact thermometers for this reason. The IR (infrared) Non-contact thermometer is meant for measuring surface temperatures from a remote location. It shoots an infrared beam out to an object and bounces to the unit and gives the temperature reading. I have seen, first hand, investigators using this thermometer as a way to measure air temperature. NO, this is not correct! Enough said. In an email conversation that I have had with Grant Wilson from TAPS, he has said that, "Any change in temperature that can't be measured with your hand is not worth notating…"

Bibliography

Belanger, Jeff. *Encyclopedia of Haunted Places.* Franklin Lakes, NJ: The Career Press, 2005.

Cahill, Robert Ellis. *Lighthouse Mysteries of the North Atlantic.* Salem, MA: Old Saltbox Publishing, 1998.

Cahill, Robert Ellis. *Ghostly Haunts.* Peabody, MA: Chandler Smith Publishing, 1983.

Hauck, Dennis William. *The National Directory of Haunted Places.* New York, NY: Penguin Books, 1996.

Jasper, Mark. *Haunted Inns of New England.* Yarmouth Port, MA: On Cape Publications, 2000.

Pitkin, David J. *Ghosts of the Northeast.* Salem, NY: Aurora Publications, 2002.

Smitten, Susan. *Ghost Stories of New England.* Auburn, WA: Lone Pine Publishing, 2003.

Smith, Terry L. and Jean, Mark. *Haunted Inns of America.* Crane Hill Publishers, 2003.

Thompson, William O. *Coastal Ghosts and Folklore.* Kennebunk, ME: Scapes Me, 2001.

Index

Haunted Rhode Island.
Thomas D'Agostino. Illustrated with over 60 photos, here are tales of Rhode Island hauntings, vampires, mysterious cairns, wailing brooks, and floating coffins. Haunted locations from throughout the state are included. Ghostly sailors prowl lonely docks, ambushed soldiers of centuries past wail, and a mysterious man in gray walks among tombstones. These are tales sure to chill you in the dead of night!

Size: 6" x 9"   62 b/w photos   128 pp.
ISBN: 0-7643-2350-4   soft cover $12.95

Connecticut Ghosts: Spirits in the State of Steady Habits. Elaine M. Kuzmeskus. Explore 31 of Connecticut's most haunted sites! On this spectral tour encounter ghosts in famous homes, including the residences of Mark Twain and Harriet Beecher Stowe. The lively spirits in Hartford, Fairfield, Litchfield County, Middlesex, New Haven, New London, and Windham County are all revealed, along with a devilish encounter in Tolland. Thirty-two images provide evidence of spirits moving among us.

Size: 6" x 9"   32 b/w photos   128 pp.
ISBN: 0-7643-2361-X   soft cover $9.95

Ghostly Beacons: Haunted Lighthouses of North America. Therese Lanigan-Schmidt. A hundred years after their deaths, meet keepers who still keep the lights burning, their spurned lovers, wronged wives, and bereaved mothers. Travel round the borders of this great country, visiting the remote lighthouses and learn the grisly tales of disastrous deaths and unsolved murders, lost loves, and hurrendous storms.

Size: 6" x 9"   33 b&w photos   160 pp.
Index
ISBN: 0-7643-1114-X   soft $14.95

Ghosts! Washington Revisited: The Ghostlore of the Nation's Capitol. John Alexander. A reporter for the Washington Star newspaper wrote in 1891, "Washington is the greatest town for ghosts in this country." Here is a collection of tales and over 180 images of famous personalities who revisit the White House, the U.S. Capitol, and other Virginia, Maryland and Washington buildings and homes said to be haunted. It is a revised and updated edition of Ghosts! Washington's Most Famous Ghost Stories.

Size: 8 1/2" x 11"   180+ b/w photo-   128 pp.
                         graphs and illustrations
ISBN: 0-7643-0653-7   soft cover $14.95

Baltimore's Harbor Haunts: True Ghost Stories. Melissa Rowell & Amy Lynwander. This spellbinding book exposes some of Baltimore, Maryland's unknown histories and uncovers 37 hauntings along the water. From the ghost of a drowned boy in Canton to famous ghosts of Fort McHenry, these tantalizing stories pay homage to the more "spirited" residents of the Canton, Fell's Point, Inner Harbor, Federal Hill and Locust Point neighborhoods.

Size: 6" x 9"   68 b/w photos   160 pp.
ISBN: 0-7643-2304-0   soft cover $14.95

Ghosts of Anchor Bay. Debi Chestnut and Linda Sparkman. Journey into haunted houses and byways of Anchor Bay, Michigan. Through 20 tales and short stories, meet the spirits, travel the roads, and enter the homes and cemeteries of Anchor Bay residents and guests. 36 color photographs. Share thrilling tales that proclaim Anchor Bay to be haunted.

Size: 6" x 9"   36 color photos   96 pp.
ISBN: 0-7643-2302-4   soft cover $9.95